Building a Career in Cyberpsychology

Building a Career in Cyberpsychology offers an accessible introduction to the various ways that cyberpsychology can be applied to different types of careers. It is designed to support individuals who are interested in applying cyberpsychology subject knowledge within their career journeys.

From consumer insights, to cyber-defence, to digital strategy, this book explores how cyberpsychology can underpin issues, challenges, and opportunities in these contexts. At the heart of all these careers is a critical understanding about how human factors can be understood and applied within digitally mediated environments. Cyberpsychology pioneer Professor Linda K. Kaye introduces readers to the fascinating field of cyberpsychology, and how our interactions with technology and the online world can help us understand the digitally connected human experience. Each chapter provides a walk-through of different types of cyberpsychologically informed careers, revealing the ways in which the digitally connected human experience is fundamental to helping us flourish in a 21st century digitalised society.

As an evidence-based, practice-oriented guide, *Building a Career in Cyberpsychology* is essential reading for students and professionals considering starting or furthering their career using cyberpsychology.

Linda K. Kaye is a Professor of Psychology in the Department of Psychology at Edge Hill University, UK. She is an expert in the broad area of cyberpsychology, the psychology of technology use and online behaviour, and has published extensively in this area. She is a founding member of the British Psychological Society Cyberpsychology Section. She is also the owner and Director of the consultancy business, The CyberDoctor® where she uses cyberpsychology subject knowledge to support organisations to enhance user-centred approaches to digital challenges.

BPS Pathways in Psychology Series
British Psychological Society

Routledge, in partnership with the British Psychological Society (BPS), is pleased to present *BPS Pathways in Psychology*, a new generation of informative books designed to support individuals looking to begin careers in or using psychology. Divided into two streams, the series offers titles both for those looking to follow a more traditional career route, or those who wish to understand how their psychology degree can inform their career outside a chartered role.

Making it clear that there is not a "one size fits all" approach to a career in or using psychology, each book is supported by case studies that highlight diversity of voice and progression routes, anecdotal guidance on avoiding pitfalls, and further reading and resources.

These early career "bookshelf essential" texts provide accessible, evidence-based, practice-oriented guides for students and professionals.

Building a Career as a Psychological Practitioner
Elspeth Ward and Kirsty McNeilis

Building a Career in Cyberpsychology
Linda K. Kaye

For more information about this series, please visit: https://www.routledge.com/our-products/book-series/BPSPIP

Building a Career in Cyberpsychology

Linda K. Kaye

Routledge
Taylor & Francis Group
LONDON AND NEW YORK

Designed cover image: Nigel Turner

First published 2027
by Routledge
4 Park Square, Milton Park, Abingdon, Oxon OX14 4RN

and by Routledge
605 Third Avenue, New York, NY 10158

Routledge is an imprint of the Taylor & Francis Group, an informa business

British Library Cataloguing-in-Publication Data
A catalogue record for this book is available from the British Library

ISBN: 9781032947761 (hbk)
ISBN: 9781032947747 (pbk)
ISBN: 9781003581741 (ebk)

DOI: 10.4324/9781003581741

Typeset in Optima
by KnowledgeWorks Global Ltd.

Contents

Tables and figures

Tables

Figures

Acronym decoder

Acronym	*Term*	*Description*
AI	Artificial intelligence	Artificial intelligence is a technology that allows computers to perform tasks that are usually done by humans
A Level	Advanced level	A-levels are qualifications that are taken in the UK to prepare for university, further study, training, or work. They are subject-based and are typically assessed by exams
B3	B3	This relates to a specific descriptor referring to "Student Outcomes" against which UK universities are measured and ranked nationally. This consists of metrics relating to the proportion of graduates from a given course who have progressed into professional employment, further study or other positive outcomes 15 months following graduation
CPD	Continued professional development	The process of learning and developing new skills and knowledge to help improve professional competence. This might include attending workshops and online courses, as well as informal learning like mentoring and on-the-job training.

(Continued)

(Continued)

Acronym	*Term*	*Description*
HCI	Human–computer interaction	Human–computer interaction is a field of study centred on optimising how users interact with systems
HE	Higher Education	A type of tertiary education (or third-level, third-stage, post-secondary education). Providers of higher education are typically universities but HE can also be delivered in Further Education colleges.
HF	Human Factors	Human Factors refers to the interaction between people and machines/systems/organisations. By understanding the human aspect of these, this helps ensure that environments are designed in a way which complements human capabilities, to maximise performance and/or safety
I-O Psychology	Industrial-Organisational Psychology	Industrial and Organisational Psychology relates to the human aspects of work lives or occupational issues. This is centred around understanding and optimising health, well-being, and effectiveness of individuals and organisations.
L&D	Learning and Development	A strategic process used by organisations to improve employee skills, knowledge, and performance. It can include activities such as training programs, workshops, and coaching to help employees grow professionally and align with the company's goals.
OfS	Office for Students	The Office for Students is an executive non-departmental public body, sponsored by the Department for Education. It acts as the regulator and competition authority for the higher education sector in England.

(Continued)

(Continued)

Acronym	*Term*	*Description*
	Marketing funnel (sometimes referred to as "purchase funnel")	A term used in marketing and advertising. The purchase cycle consumers go through from awareness to loyalty
	Post-16	Post-16 education is any type of education or training that takes place after a person turns 16 years old. It includes further education, such as college or apprenticeships, and higher education, such as university.
	Sixth form	Sixth form is a term used in the UK to represent the final two years of secondary education, ages 16 to 18. Pupils typically prepare for A-level or equivalent examinations
TEF	Teaching Excellence Framework	The Teaching Excellence Framework is a UK scheme hosted by the Office for Students (OfS). This is built around the ambition of ensuring that higher education providers are delivering excellence in teaching and learning, and in student outcomes (e.g., graduate earnings, graduate-level jobs). This is an assessment which rates universities and colleges based on a set of requirements for quality and standards.
UCD	User-centred design	A design process in which designers focus on the users and their needs as being central to the way systems are designed and implemented
UX	User Experience	This refers to what users experience when using a product, application, system, or service. This might include how well they can navigate a system, its ease of use, how personalised it is and so on. This might include consumer insights or user testing as part of evaluating user needs.

(Continued)

(Continued)

Acronym	*Term*	*Description*
VR	Virtual Reality	A technology that exposes the user to a computer-generated environment and makes it possible to interact with it in a very realistic way. It is often experienced by the user through them wearing a headset.

Chapter 1

Introduction

Psychology as an academic subject is consistently shown to be a popular choice for those in post-16 education. Indeed, at the point where students can select the subjects they wish to study in sixth form or college, psychology has been among the top subjects consistently over the last few decades. Within the UK alone, psychology remains among the top three subjects selected at A-level (FTT Education Data Lab, 2025) and applications to psychology courses at university have ranged from 138,055 to 154,900 over the last five years (UCAS, 2025). This yields a significant number of psychology graduates every year, who are entering the workforce, most with ambitions to directly apply psychology in their career. The popularity of psychology as a post-16 study option is largely reflected globally too, with increasing trends being evident in the number of total psychology bachelor degrees awarded in the USA (APA, 2023). Specifically, in 2023, 140,711 psychology bachelor degrees were awarded in US institutions (APA, 2023).

Perhaps one of the most fascinating attributes of psychology is its sheer breadth as a subject of study. Indeed, we can understand human thought and behaviour from a multitude of perspectives, drawing on a wide range of theories and methodologies. Not only is its nature rather broad, but its applications are equally diverse and varied. Whilst there is often a tendency to assume that the primary purpose of a psychology degree is to become a practitioner as a "Psychologist", this is intriguingly far from the realities of how psychology graduates tend to apply their subject knowledge in careers. Chapter 2 will elaborate more on this issue, and provide some insight into what these various types of careers might be. Broadly, we might use the term "psychologically

DOI: 10.4324/9781003581741-1

informed" career as a reference point for what these relevant, yet diverse career routes might be.

Cyberpsychology is perhaps one such psychologically informed career pathway. That is, there is not a practitioner-route in this domain and it certainly is not the case that there is a registered title of "Cyberpsychologist" which can be conferred by any health councils. However, there are a multitude of ways in which cyberpsychology subject knowledge and skills can be applied in career roles. Chapter 3 will provide some general overview of what these can be, and each chapter thereafter will illuminate more specifically some thematic areas in which cyberpsychology has been applied.

Cyberpsychology in its broadest sense is the psychology of technology use and online behaviour. Essentially, it can help us understand the digitally connected human experience. In the context of the 21st century, in which most of our everyday interactions and experiences consist of some form of digital technology or element of online connectivity, the relevance of cyberpsychology should not be under-stated. Indeed, we have a clear need to understand the intersections of technology and connectivity in a wide range of domains such as: communication and socialisation, work and productivity, learning and education, lifestyle and well-being, legal proceedings and public protection, and business and transactions, to name a few. Chapter 3 will provide a more substantive definition of cyberpsychology and the various topics which can be studied within this subject to provide additional context about how this relates to cyberpsychology career pathways.

Whilst we might like to work under the assumption that people want to study psychology because they are simply fascinated by the subject, I cannot help but feel there are other more prominent characteristics of the current zeitgeist of motivations for study. It has become more evident that in the UK context at least, career options and ambitions are more central to students' selection of subjects at university, perhaps over the intrinsic value of the subject itself. Within UK higher education, there have been Governmental-led initiatives within the last decade which have arguably driven this more exclusive focus on university-level study as a utilitarian pursuit for career outcomes. I would argue that there are two key initiatives which have driven this, particularly within the UK context: i) UK tuition fee increases, and ii) higher education institutional excellence being determined by graduate outcomes.

The first point relates to Government-determined tuition fees in 2012, in most of the UK, being increased approximately three-fold in excess of £9,000 per year for full-time study. This has been attributed to more utilitarian-based motivations for attending university and in determining choices about subject area (Kaye & Bates, 2014). Specifically, people's decisions on which subject area to study at university-level became more focused on the tangible outcomes associated with courses such as career opportunities and potential graduate earnings. As such, electing a subject at university has gradually become more occupied in discourse around careers and less perhaps about passion or intrinsic interest in a subject area and studying it for its own sake. This is regrettable but a direct consequence of the economical shifts within UK higher education.

In relation to the second point, this refers to the way UK Higher Education is regulated. Whilst in former years, universities were overseen by the Higher Education Academy (HEA), which focused on improving teaching and learning, this was superseded by the Office for Students (OfS) in 2018. The OfS is a non-departmental public body of the Department for Education which acts as the regulator and competition authority for the higher education sector in England. In respect of its relationship towards more career-focused outcomes, the OfS places significant emphasis on measuring institutional excellence based on graduate outcomes (e.g., graduate earnings, proportion of graduates in graduate level employment several months after graduation). Specifically, the Teaching Excellence Framework (TEF) includes Condition B3 which specifies graduate outcomes as a condition for determining institutional teaching excellence. It is not surprising then that UK higher education institutions are motivated to prioritise career-related provision and marketing as a routine part of providing study options. Arguably, these Government-level drivers have had a direct impact on academic subject areas such as psychology. In response, we have seen universities more explicitly aligning curricula to employability and career-related provision, and professional bodies such as the British Psychological Society investing in diversifying their career resource offer. Indeed, this book is itself one of many resources which extends this offer, in this case, towards increasing awareness of "psychologically informed" career pathways.

Whilst these aforementioned might be exclusive to UK or English-based psychology providers, there are additional considerations for cyberpsychology careers, more specifically. One such driver, which I would argue applies globally, is the increased focus on "cyber" or digital within industrial strategy. Specifically, this relates to Governmental industrial strategy regarding digital innovation. UK examples include: the National Cyber Strategy 2022, and the UK Government's Digital Strategy both of which place emphasis on ensuring the UK remains competitive in business and innovation in a "fast-moving digital world". Given that this is becoming a central priority in most, if not all, Government-level industrial policy, globally, it is not surprising that there are investments and resources being placed upon cyber careers, to support Government sectors in responding to these priorities.

This book is situated as a way of outlining examples which illustrate how cyberpsychology can be applied to forge psychologically informed career pathways. The book is structured around four main themes: consumer cyberpsychology, health cyberpsychology, industrial-organisational cyberpsychology, and forensic cyberpsychology. These specific thematic areas were selected as they are the most prominent areas in which cyberpsychology tends to be explicitly used or discussed in respect of career applications; however, they should not be considered a complete list of options. Each thematic chapter consists of the following structural approach: introduction, outline and definition of the theme, prominent issues, Case Studies, advice, and further resources. It is designed to be as practically useful as possible, and might inspire those interested in cyberpsychology to consider the wide range of ways it can be applied within careers. Additionally, this book also includes more generic guidance regarding cyberpsychology careers, such as advice towards becoming a consultant or founding a cyberpsychology-related business. Whilst the book is not designed as a comprehensive resource in this regard, some key insights are complementary to the discussion about how cyberpsychology can function as part of a range of different career ambitions.

Resources

British Psychological Society (2024). *Find your career in psychology*. Retrieved October 15, 2024, from: https://www.bps.org.uk/find-your-career-psychology

Office for Students (nd). *Condition B3: baselines for student outcomes indicators*. Retrieved October 15, 2024, from: https://www.officeforstudents.org.uk/media/490d884f-03aa-49cf-907d-011149309983/condition_b3_baselines.pdf

UCAS (2025). *Psychology Subject Guide*. Retrieved September 11, 2025, from https://www.ucas.com/explore/subjects/psychology

References

APA (American Psychological Association). (2022). *Degrees in psychology*. Retrieved October 16, 2025, from https://www.apa.org/workforce/data-tools/degrees-psychology

FTT Education Data Lab (2025). *Which A-Level subjects are the most popular?* Retrieved August 1, 2025, from https://ffteducationdatalab.org.uk/2022/08/which-a-level-subjects-are-the-most-popular/

Kaye, L. K., & Bates, E. A. (2014). The impact of higher fees on students' reasons for attending university. *Journal of Further and Higher Education, 41*(3), 379–392. https://doi.org/10.1080/0309877X.2015.1117597

UCAS (2025). UCAS *Undergraduate end of cycle data resources 2024*. Retrieved August 1, 2025, from https://www.ucas.com/data-and-analysis/undergraduate-statistics-and-reports/ucas-undergraduate-end-cycle-data-resources-2024

Chapter 2

Being a psychology graduate

Psychology graduate routes

As noted in Chapter 1, psychology as an academic subject is consistently shown to be a popular choice within post-16 education. This yields a significant number of psychology graduates every year who are entering the workforce, most with ambitions to directly apply psychology in their career. Whilst it might typically be assumed that the primary purpose of a psychology degree is to become a practitioner as a "Psychologist", only a minority of psychology graduates actually pursue psychology practitioner careers such as in Forensic Psychology, Clinical Psychology, and so on. There can be various reasons for this. Firstly, with respect to the practitioner training routes in psychology, the combination of high graduate demand for these opportunities, but low availability of course places at a small number of provider institutions can prove to be a major barrier. Relatedly, this means that places on these training programmes are highly competitive and so this might not be a viable option for many prospective applicants. Secondly, the prospect of several additional years of training following an undergraduate degree can be off-putting for graduates who might instead seek jobs as a means of generating income. This might be particularly relevant in nations which have high interest rates on student loans, where graduates might be discouraged from taking on additional course fees and potential debt. Finally, some graduates become enlightened on their psychology course about the range of other career opportunities which might be relevant to them. Some of these might relate to "psychologically informed" careers, which will be discussed next.

DOI: 10.4324/9781003581741-2

Before defining "psychologically informed careers", it is important to first outline what constitutes "traditional" professions in psychology. Traditional psychology professions could be considered to be those which follow formal professional training programmes. This might typically involve accredited postgraduate and/or doctoral level study and supervised practice, whereby one's respective Psychologist title is regulated as a protected title by the Health and Care Professions Council (HCPC). This route relates to the following practitioner pathways: Clinical, Child/Educational, Forensic, Health, Counselling, Neuropsychology, Occupational, Sport and Exercise, and Coaching. However, there might be many people who use psychology in their careers, but do not consider themselves to be a "psychologist". These are careers which might be best considered as being "psychologically informed careers".

Some examples of psychologically informed careers might include: consumer psychology, environmental/climate psychology, community psychology, and of course, cyberpsychology. The diversity of psychologically informed careers relates not only to the domain/field of interest but also the type of sector or organisation and job title. It might be that roles refer to "behavioural science" or similar, and so might not even specifically make reference to "psychology" in respect of the role. However, in careers where the focus is on understanding human thought and/or behaviour, whether that be understanding attitudes and perceptions, motivating behaviour, or changing behaviour, these are likely careers which have at least some element of being "psychologically informed". A key distinction between being a "psychologist" within psychologically informed careers relative to more standard psychology careers is that because the former does not follow an established practitioner training route, opportunities may be available at graduate entry (rather than exclusively at postgraduate level). Additionally, being a Psychologist within a psychologically informed career may often be as a result of being situated within an organisation and being aligned towards its needs rather than being a Psychologist from a more generic training pathway. An example of this is a Psychologist within a social enterprise for climate change education. A Psychologist here might operate alongside a team of campaign managers, commissioners, bid writers, or researchers. In this case, the Psychologist's role is to understand how to motivate behaviour change, change attitudes, and other things relating to climate change education. This role does not necessitate that they have achieved a protected psychologist title conferred via specified training routes, but instead that they have suitable psychology-related subject knowledge, qualifications, experience and skills which relate to their role and contributions within the organisation.

These distinctions in being a Psychologist clearly can "muddy the water" in respect of how psychologists are perceived by the general public and how they are regulated. Essentially, a psychology graduate who secures a job of a "Psychologist" within an organisation may use this title but this is somewhat distinctive from a "Clinical Psychologist", for example, who has completed doctoral-level training and is registered with the HCPC. This is not to say that psychologically informed career pathways as a "Psychologist" are not valuable, but rather that caution should be warranted to avoid mis-representing one's credentials.

Attributes of being a psychology graduate

Being a psychology graduate has significant currency for a number of reasons. Firstly, it synergises insights about "people" together with the "science", which very few other subjects do. Here, we not only gain insights about human-centred experiences and approaches, but we remain empirically and scientifically grounded in research enquiry, and use of evidence and data for understanding human thought and behaviour. From a utilitarian perspective, this potentially offers a wide range of opportunities for graduate careers. Secondly, in respect of specific types of skills, because undergraduate psychology courses typically include a significant amount of research methods and analysis training, psychology graduates have a suitable skill-set to apply to activities which might apply to many organisations such as evaluation, research and development, processing and analysing data, using data software, and using data and evidence to inform decision-making. These sorts of activities might be critical to helping organisations fulfil their strategic objectives and help them answer questions such as:

- What are our customers' attitudes towards our products/ services? (And are these positive enough to ensure our business is sustainable in its current form?)

- How effective is our sustainability awareness-campaign? (And is it worth us continuing to resource this?)
- How can we better engage with our clients? (And can this enhance our success as a business?)

As such, research and data skills are critical to knowing the most suitable methods for collecting these types of data, analysing and interpreting them, and using them appropriately to inform organisational decision-making. In relation to cyberpsychology more specifically, added benefits of psychology graduates with cyberpsychology knowledge include: designing studies to reach specific online populations, handling and understanding digital trace data or online data, understanding biases and challenges in online samples, and understanding ethics and professional standards relating to internet-mediated research. Related to research is ethics. Whilst psychology graduates will routinely have a solid understanding of ethical standards and practices in undertaking research and handling data, additional attributes of cyberpsychology graduates include: understanding how to best operationalise consent and anonymity online, the impacts of AI on bias, and ethics relating to persuasive or manipulative technology or systems.

Finally, attributes associated with being a psychology graduate include having a sound understanding of human-centred experiences, which can be helpful for offering more stratified or personalised strategies. Whilst this is commonly discussed in areas of education and health, such as personalised education provision or personalised treatment plans, respectively, these principles apply more widely. For example, understanding demographic or personality profiles can be informative for designing more tailored communication or campaigns, which can extend not only within the communication sector but also in any type of organisation which seeks to communicate effectively with clients, customers, trustees, stakeholders or beneficiaries. Clearly, this has relevance to a wide range of organisations and career roles.

Putting the "cyber" in psychology careers

Whilst psychology subject knowledge has significant value to a wide range of careers, I argue that cyberpsychology as a specific domain of psychology is especially well situated to tackle 21st century global issues. This can include; supporting digital transformation, tackling digital poverty, integrating the use of AI and automation, and much more. Indeed, for psychology graduates who have subject knowledge relating to cyberpsychology, this might present them with a competitive edge within the job market. This has the potential to extend a wide range of sectors, industries and job roles. To give a brief indication of how "digital" can relate to a wide range of sectors and industries, Table 2.1 includes some indicative examples.

Within these sectors, there might be a wide range of job roles and titles used, and in many cases, roles will not always be specific in responding to these indicative challenges. As such, it is not necessarily a straightforward task to find cyberpsychologically informed job roles. The subsequent chapters provide some

Table 2.1 Indicative types of digital challenges for different sectors and industries

Sector/Organisation	*Indicative digital challenges*
Public sector – health	Digital health transformation, implementation, innovation, data privacy, data analytics and AI, patient access/inclusion, digital twins
Public sector – education	Harnessing digital data (e.g., pupil data), digital transformation and innovation, digital upskilling and training, AI in professional practice, AI to support learning
Corporate sector	Cybersecurity threats, digital transformation, managing remote/hybrid working, environmental digital impact
Commercial and retail sector	Optimising digital marketing, handling digital consumer and transaction data, seamless consumer experience, omnichannel integration and consumer mapping, timely consumer (online) relations, understanding the role of AI in the consumer experience
Communications sector	Developing a connectivity ecosystem, understanding the intersection of AI in digital communication
Industrial sector	Cyber risks, ensuring operational continuity and supply chain resilience
Manufacturing and construction	Robust supply chain management, sustainability initiatives, handling the threat of job displacement due to automation

(Continued)

Table 2.1 (Continued)

Sector/Organisation	*Indicative digital challenges*
Defence and security sector	Awareness of rapidly evolving attacks, understanding complex regulatory landscapes, integrating emerging technologies into systems, use of AI within cyber-attacks, understanding nuances of how online spaces affect human behaviour and potential cyber perpetration and vulnerability
Legal sector	Understanding complex regulatory landscapes, data confidentiality and data protection, digital verification
Financial sector	Navigating regulatory landscapes, advertising regulations digital transformation, cybersecurity threats and fraudulent activity, adopting blockchain, demands for mobile banking
Hospitality and leisure	(Online) Customer relationship management, seamless personalised experience, digital representation

indicative job roles and keywords which can help in this regard, particularly when careers might relate to particular thematic areas.

However, as a general guide, "behavioural scientist" or similar might often be used within public sector recruitment or Government-led agencies (e.g., such as defence and security). These are well suited to psychology graduates including those with cyberpsychology subject knowledge, especially if they are situated in organisations which have a digital focus (e.g., online education, digital health, cybersecurity) or remit surrounding digital transformation. Conversely, within other sectors, it might be less common for them to have designated roles within organisations, and instead they might be more inclined to buy-in expertise in the form of external consultancy as and when this might be required. With this in mind, Chapter 3 includes advice and practical guidance on how to become a consultant.

How cyberpsychology can tackle key challenges

On a more general level, there are societal challenges which might apply across a range of sectors, organisations, and society more widely. Whist psychology is well-suited to informing many global issues, such as improving health and well-being, building more inclusive societies, and so on, cyberpsychology may present an additional edge in this respect.

Health and well-being

Psychological insight can be extremely valuable in supporting physical and psychological health, as is evidenced from the fact we have domains such as Health Psychology and Sport and Exercise Psychology. However, given the significant ambition towards digital transformation within health services, there are perhaps useful insights which cyberpsychology can contribute here. Specifically, this might apply at any individual patient or health practitioner level whereby insight from user experience (UX) might explain how or why individuals might struggle to engage with using certain digital tools or services. In general, psychological insight within the digital health realm can be helpful to understand things such as: how to make support more accessible via digital or online services or tools, understand how to personalise support or interventions, and explore the role of different types of therapeutic interactions (e.g., AI-assisted therapy). It might also apply on a wider organisational level to encourage digital transformation and innovation within health services or trusts, whereby insights from technology acceptance might inform key barriers to digital health tool or service adoption. As such, there may be specific insights which cyberpsychology subject knowledge can contribute beyond more general psychology domain expertise. More specific insights on Health Cyberpsychology are detailed in Chapter 5.

Inclusive society

Whilst there are a wide range of psychological principles that can be applied to promoting inclusion (e.g., reducing bias, building collective identity, imagined social contact, etc.), there might be specific considerations when inclusion has a digital component. This can include fundamental aspects such as access and connectivity, as well as skills and capabilities of using services and tools. Further, this can extend to literacy in using online interactions and behaviours, and their relationship to social norms within certain (online) contexts and communities. These represent multiple layers of what being "digitally inclusive" can refer to, and require specific subject knowledge ranging from ICT or technical (in the case of initial access and connectivity issues), to those which are more cyberpsychological, in order to apply differently to these constituent issues. In the latter case, cyberpsychological knowledge can be helpful for understanding things like how online behaviours relate to identity expressions and disclosure, and how the nature of behaviours and interactions relate to online community engagement and effectiveness. All these are characteristics associated with digital inclusion, but within policy and practice the focus tends to be more exclusively on the more technical aspects of access. Whilst this is clearly important, there are far more comprehensive insights which can be derived from disciplines such as from cyberpsychology, to underpin how (online) behaviours themselves relate to inclusivity.

Some specific issues might relate to how individuals construct and express identities and in-groups within digital spaces in respect of what markers and behaviours are used to signal these identities. There might also be different cues that out-groups might use in digital spaces, which forge how intergroup biases are realised. As such, understanding how online and digital behaviour corresponds to both individual and social processes is of critical importance to supporting more inclusive (digital) societies and communities.

Understanding (digital) engagement

"Engagement" is a widely used term which has many facets, including cognitive, emotional and behavioural dimensions. However, in respect of digital or online engagement this term can equally be used somewhat interchangeably, and include many components. In one sense, "engagement" might refer simply to the behavioural act or specific interactions which take place on a device or when using a software. This might typically be what is focused on in the realm of user experience and interaction practices. However, the terms online or digital engagement might also be used to more generally refer to our general patterns or tendencies towards using digital/online products or services (e.g., "Sally is highly engaged on social media").

There are many cross-sector challenges which are focused on "engagement" such as how to engage youth in young people services, how to optimise online engagement in consumer marketing, how to engage the general public in charitable campaigns, how to encourage patients to engage with healthy lifestyle advice, how to encourage attendance and engagement in school, and so on. Each of these are focused on "engagement" yet are arguably not all referring to the same thing. Why is this relevant? Take the example of youth engagement. A key challenge for many youth services might be how to encourage young people to engage in services which provide them with community or educational activities to develop personal, social and professional skills, support well-being, and generally offer a nurturing environment, particularly for those who might be considered vulnerable. Post-COVID, there has been a general observation that people are drawn more towards online options to engage with educational, social and/or vocational activities, and so youth services might consider online programmes to be a potential opportunity for encouraging engagement. However, this brings up a potential challenge: what should this online alternative look like in terms of format to encourage "engagement" from young people? For example, should it include self-paced units, or perhaps include online synchronised provision? There can be issues here which cyberpsychological subject knowledge can start to answer, with regards to digital interactions and behaviour, and how this varies across different types of online environments. However, this is a somewhat different question than the more general issue of encouraging "engagement" (i.e. which might relate more to inclination or uptake of services) which is perhaps the more inherent and critical issue.

When considering the range of cross-sector challenges that relate to (dis)engagement, it is important to recognise that introduction of digital or online formats is not necessarily a silver bullet to solve this issue. Introducing an app into patient services will not magically encourage patients to eat healthier or exercise more; having a charity website will not in itself encourage people to give more money. As such, although cyberpsychology knowledge can help address the more specific interaction behaviours or behavioural components related to "digital engagement", this has to be considered in the context of the underpinning psychological or emotional components related to engagement, which require more complex solutions. Indeed, psychology as a discipline more generally can be well placed to support on this endeavour.

Digital adoption and transformation

Whilst Occupational Psychologists, sometimes referred to as Industrial-Organisational Psychologists, might typically be well placed to support organisational change, support people and culture, and oversee change management programmes, cyberpsychological insight might be useful for things such as organisational digital transformation or optimisation. These sorts of organisational transformations might benefit from more specified intervention programmes or tools, drawing on principles from technology acceptance, or even user experience perspectives. Examples include change programmes which bring in new employee management systems or similar, in which understanding the usability and acceptability of such systems for replacing or complementing existing processes may determine the success of organisational management within a company. These can therefore be more specified towards understanding the challenges at hand around the digital–human interactions rather than perhaps being more generalised people engagement and management interventions. The same applies to the integration of AI or automation within organisations, whereby having more specialised subject insight into the nature of interactions between humans and digital can make transformation programmes more bespoke to these specific challenges. Some further examples relating to Industrial-Organisational Cyberpsychology are provided in Chapter 6.

The above are just some indicative examples of how cyberpsychology knowledge might be well suited to complement the types of insights which psychologists might typically contribute. I argue that we are at a time within society where we are faced with a range of digital challenges, all of which cyberpsychology graduates can be well placed to tackle. The later chapters of this book focus on domain-specific issues, and provide an overview of the ways in which cyberpsychological insights might relate to these.

Resources

APA (American Psychological Association). Careers in Applied Psychology Webinar Series – https://www.apa.org/education-career/training/careers-applied-psychology-series

APA (American Psychological Association). Careers in Applied Psychology Playlist – https://www.youtube.com/playlist?list=PLxf85IzktYWJWkSMebi12JEQvxZbpQ0AM

BPS (British Psychological Society). Career Options in Psychology – https://www.bps.org.uk/career-options-in-psychology

Chapter 3

Cyberpsychology careers

What is cyberpsychology?

Cyberpsychology, in its broadest sense, is the psychology of technology use and online behaviour. Essentially, it can help us understand the digitally-connected human experience. In the context of the 21st century, in which most of our everyday interactions and experiences consist of some form of digital technology or element of online connectivity, the relevance of cyberpsychology should not be under-estimated. Indeed, we have a clear need to understand the intersections of technology and connectivity in a wide range of domains such as: communication and socialisation, work and productivity, learning and education, lifestyle and well-being, legal proceedings and public protection, and business and transactions, to name a few. As such, cyberpsychology and the insights which can be garnered about online behaviour, can present highly insightful perspectives which can be applied to many 21st century societal challenges and opportunities.

But what do we mean by online behaviour? Arguably, this can refer to lots of different things based on the diverse ways we use connected technology. We have defined three types of online behaviour as: online-exclusive behaviour, online-mediated behaviour, and online-recorded behaviour (Kaye et al., 2022). Online-exclusive behaviour refers to any behaviour which natively occurs in a digital form, such as typing, scrolling, and posting photos on social media. These are behaviours which would not exist without an internet-enabled device. Online-mediated behaviours are natural behaviours which occur in the "offline" world but which are communicated via connected technology such as

DOI: 10.4324/9781003581741-3

videochat or streaming. As such the behaviour itself occurs in the physical world but it is the technology which communicates this to others. Finally, online-recorded behaviours occur in the physical world but the communication of them is captured in an alternative format such as metrics. An example of this would be fitness apps which record walking behaviour (which the user undertakes "naturally" in their physical world) but the communication of this is captured in a different format such as numerically (e.g., miles walked).

Why is this important? We tend to assume that "online behaviour" is simply behaviour which is exclusive to, and occurs natively on digital platforms. However, in an increasingly connected world, we should also be cognisant of the fact that there are clear intersections of the digital with our "offline" behaviours and physical worlds. As such, the diversity of behaviours which might sit under "cyberpsychology" can be very broad and all-encompassing. Behaviours which occur in our physical world such as movement behaviours can be captured via internet-enabled digital devices such as smart doorbells or smart watches, and transformed into digital data of sorts. Therefore even our "offline" behaviour can in some respects be considered a form of "online behaviour" when it is captured and represented in this way.

I would argue that there are intrinsic values of cyberpsychology when it is applied to the study of 21st century human behaviour. One of these relates to the fact that across all applications of cyberpsychology whether they be online marketing or threat detection, human factors remain central to gaining the human insight perspective into digital systems, processes, and strategies which might otherwise be absent. However, one might argue that psychology more generally might be equally capable of fulfilling this need. However, I would argue there are particular nuances with certain types of digital interactions which require more specific cyberpsychology input. Primarily, this relates to the fact that there are some behaviours which exist in the digital sphere which do not have an obvious "offline" equivalent. As such existing psychological theory simply is not able to explain these behaviours. Another merit of cyberpsychology is well suited to understand how our intersection with algorithms and artificial intelligence (AI) can forge more personalised experiences and how this, in turn, might harness more effective or satisfying human experiences in leisure, business, recreation, and service use. This presents an intriguing opportunity and corresponds to societal movements which have transitioned away from mass consumption and engagement experiences, towards personalisation and user-driven experiences.

When thinking about the general way that cyberpsychology can be applied in careers, a good starting point is to recognise the types of insights which cyberpsychology subject knowledge might have relative to what other specialist areas might offer. One such example is Human Factors (HF), discussed next.

Human Factors

Human Factors psychology (sometimes referred to as Ergonomics) explores the interactions between humans and elements of a system. This broadly applies principles and methods from psychology or other relevant disciplines, to optimise human wellbeing and performance. Human Factors Practitioners can work in various areas such as: human–computer interaction (HCI), team communication, designing intelligent tutoring systems, threat detection, management consultancy. HF is readily applied in organisational contexts, especially from the perspective of optimising performance and productivity, but equally can be applied in any setting which benefits from understanding the "human" intersection of systems.

Cyberpsychology careers broadly apply the principles of HF with respect to gaining insight into the "human" element of a system or issue, but more specifically, would more typically apply these to understand human behaviours which occur within or as a result of digital systems. An example here might be threat detection in cybersecurity, rather than the security sector more generally. That is, whilst HF might be able to gain insight into the predictors of security risks in the "offline" world, there may be specific insights into the predictors or correlates of online or digital behaviours which cyberpsychology could offer here.

The value of cyberpsychology

In addition to the aforementioned general benefits about adopting a human factors perspective to technology and systems, there are some more specific perspectives that cyberpsychology can bring to businesses or industry in respect of digital infrastructure and operations. These are outlined in the following sections.

Firstly, whilst policies and practices often treat people as the "problem" or the weakest link in technical systems, cyberpsychology instead recognises that there are factors which can be targeted to better understand these vulnerabilities. These might include how users can behave irrationally when faced with extreme cognitive load or stress or when undertaking tasks or behaviours that have become habitual or automatic. As such, digital use is so much more than just a technical exercise; and we should be cognisant that psychological resilience principles are critical to integrate at an individual and organisational level, to reduce cyber risk or failures. Additionally, cybersecurity strategies should build on human tendencies in habit-formation and use behavioural nudges as suitable techniques for encouraging appropriate security-relevant behaviours. Human factors relating to cybersecurity-related issues are discussed further in Chapter 7.

Secondly, cyberpsychology helps us understand the nature and novelties of digital or online behaviours relative to those we may be more familiar with in the physical world. Additionally, in a consumer context, knowing how digital behaviours correspond to users, their characteristics and other psychological correlates are valuable for us to better understand consumers/customers, employees, and other relevant user groups of interest. Further, we also recognise that there may be some conditions under which people behave differently in some online formats compared to how they may do in the physical world. Indeed, principles from the Online Disinhibition Effect (Suler, 2004) can go some way to explain how factors such as perceived anonymity and asynchronicity of interactions may foster more disinhibited behaviour (Cho & Kwon, 2015; Sproull & Kiesler, 1986). Whilst this might not apply in all contexts and to all types of online behaviour, it is a valuable perspective to inform platform design and community engagement methods to ensure appropriate cultures around organisations, brands, services, and so on. This has key implications in applied domains such as marketing, communications, and product design, which are the focus of Chapter 4.

Thirdly, whilst data and analytics garnered from digital platforms and tools might help understand *what* users do, cyberpsychology can help explain *why*. For example, user engagement based on dwell time on webpages does not necessarily equate to satisfaction; instead it might relate to confusion or incomprehensibility of information. Integrating cyberpsychology into analytics can offer much more enriched insight which ultimately might result in better decision-making at an organisational level. This is relevant both in respect of understanding consumer behaviour (Chapter 4) and also in relation to employee behaviour within organisations (Chapter 6).

Finally, in relation to AI and indeed other non-human components or digital use, cyberpsychology is valuable as it illustrates how humans tend to anthropomorphise AI (Folk et al., 2025) and what the behavioural impacts of this may be. As such, this may help explain people's propensity to over-trust AI and therefore reduce rational judgement and decision-making within these interactions. This can offer some insight into *why* impacts associated with AI may occur, beyond just being able to explore *what* these impacts are. The intersection of AI into psychology is an area of current discussion. In particular, large language models are becoming integrated into the everyday practices of psychologists such as assisting in teaching, making sense of fallacies of psychological constructs, and providing a window for us to study human beliefs and cognition through the production of human-like language (Kasneci et al., 2023; Wulff & Mata, 2025). An applied example of this is through silicon sampling. Silicon samples are essentially replica participants which are created by asking a large language model to create a participant who occupies specific demographic characteristics (e.g., age, gender, race, etc/). They are asked to respond to psychological tasks in a way which mirrors how a participant with those characteristics would be expected to. When undertaken on a large scale, this produces data sets which can be argued to be representative of a population of interest. However, the efficacy of this for replicating human behaviour has been questioned given that responses tend to be far more homogeneous across samples than would be expected in a human sample. Clearly, there is a real need for more scrutiny of the way large language models, as a key type of AI, are being integrated into psychological research and practice, which signals there to be a central role for cyberpsychology in these discussions.

Case studies

I present three Case Studies which give examples of professionals who apply cyberpsychology in their respective careers. These are: Dr Inka Karppinen who is a Senior Security Culture Analyst, Bec McKeown who is the Founder and Principal Psychologist at Mind Science, and Ruth Guest who is the Founder of Sersha. All these Case Studies represent careers within businesses, primarily either in or interacting with the private sector. In most cases, the type of work involves engaging with and applying cyberpsychology evidence to use, either as part of stakeholder education, or within organisations for training and consultancy. Other Case Studies are presented throughout this book within the respective thematic chapters, and introduce a range of professionals in different job roles who each apply cyberpsychology which can offer a broader array of sectors and career roles. These are designed to give practical examples of the wide range of career roles, sectors, career pathways routes, and insights that can be contained in cyberpsychologically-informed careers.

Case study 1 Dr Inka Karppinen: Senior Security Culture Analyst at FNZ (UK) Ltd and former Lead Behavioural Scientist at CybSafe

Qualifications

- PhD. and MRes in Security and Crime Science
- MSc in Occupational Psychology

Networks

- Chartered Psychologist of British Psychological Society (BPS)
- Expert Fellow of Sprite+
- Member of Global Association of Applied Behavioural Scientists (GAABS)
- Honorary Research Fellow, Security & Crime Science, UCL

How Inka applies cyberpsychology

- Applying research knowledge to design, develop, and implement engaging security awareness and training programmes tailored to various job roles, ensuring the entire business understands the importance of cybersecurity
- Using behavioural science to encourage more secure digital and online behaviours to help protect individuals and the organisation
- Applying research knowledge to analyse and assess employee security behaviours, identify areas for improvement and implement targeted interventions and nudges to reduce human cyber risk
- Using insights from Occupational Psychology to support culture-building by integrating cyber security across the organisation's core values and work culture
- Designing culture surveys, collecting, analysing, and reporting data relating to cybersecurity attitudes and behaviours
- Managing the phishing simulation programme, including designing, analysing trends, and reporting to senior leadership
- Working collaboratively with Information Security technical colleagues to draw in communication, communicate risks, and culture perspectives into ways of working
- Providing evidence-based research and expertise in cyberpsychology to help inform product development and develop workable digital solutions. These all help the company support people make better choices and outsmart cyber threats

More information: https://www.linkedin.com/in/inkakarppinen/

Case study 2 Bec McKeown: Founder and Principal Psychologist at Mind Science

Qualifications

- MSc Applied Psychology

Networks

- Chartered Psychologist and Associate Fellow of British Psychological Society (BPS)

How Bec applies cyberpsychology

- Ensuring products are underpinned by the latest evidence-based science
- Applying principles to CPD/training programmes for defence and security professionals who work in VUCA (Volatile, Uncertain, Complex, Ambiguous) environments
- Applying insights to writing thought-leadership pieces
- Applying principles from cognitive readiness to volatility, uncertainty, complexity, and VUCA environments
- Using psychological principles to design metrics to assess human performance.
- Designing research programmes to solve complex human performance issues in the workplace

Case study 3 Ruth Guest: Photographer and Founder of Sersha

Qualifications

- MSc in Cyberpsychology

How Ruth applies cyberpsychology

- Applying her understanding of social media self-presentation combined with her knowledge in creativity to inform how people, pre-teens and adults, might navigate the online world and present themselves through computer-mediated communication (CMC)
- Designing social media training for pre-teens in the form of an interactive game

More information: https://ruthguest.com/

Routes into cyberpsychology

Given that it has been taking time for cyberpsychology to infiltrate into different sectors and industries, it is not surprising that currently there are occasions where people might only now be looking into career transitions which accommodate cyberpsychology study or training, as this might not have been available or recognised at the point of their career entry. As such, in addition to new psychology graduates, there is a much wider and more diverse market who might be well suited to cyberpsychology study and training as part of career development. These might include professionals within careers such as Marketing, IT, and Defence and Security.

A "Cyberpsychologist" is not a job role you will see very often. Cyberpsychology is often more of a lens than a single career pathway. Although not exhaustive, Figure 3.1 summarises some of the observed career trajectories which might currently typically exist within cyberpsychologically-informed career routes. These broadly can be characterised under three categories: psychology domains, consumer and organisational domains, and ICT domains. In the latter two categories, these might typically include candidates who have previous qualifications and experience in non-psychology related fields, who might be seeking insight into the human element, or aspects of human behaviour online, to help inform professional activities. As such, within-career cyberpsychology training or professional development may be sought to draw in

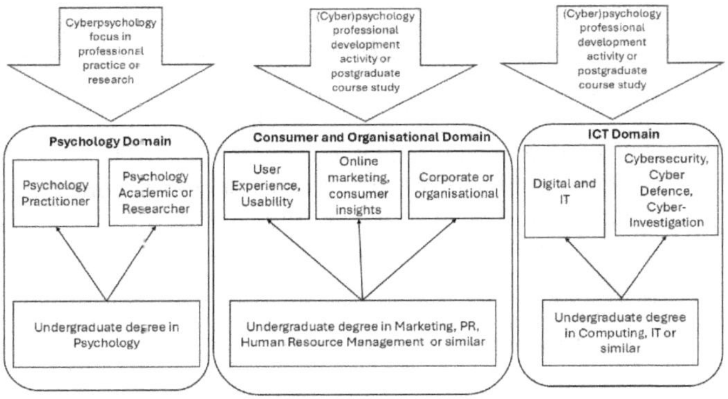

Figure 3.1 Visual of indicative career domains and how cyberpsychology training or professional development might intersect

these perspectives into professional practice. Within the psychology domain, cyberpsychology integration might more typically be in the form of scholarship or professional practice which has a focus on cyberpsychology. Whilst this does not include a comprehensive account of the wide range of pathways that any individual might take, or imply that people remain in one domain, it gives an indicative summary of the typical types of routes and themes of cyberpsychologically-informed careers which currently exist. Case Studies presented within this book provide additional examples of what types of qualifications and career roles are relevant for people currently working within cyberpsychology-related careers.

General advice

It is worth being cautious when using the term "Cyberpsychologist." The reason for this is that there is not a registered practitioner pathway in this domain. For example, in the UK, "Cyberpsychologist" is not one of the protected titles with the Health and Care Professions Council (HCPC). Similarly, in the US, licensure regulation prevents this term being used. Using the term "Cyberpsychologist" may bring on the perception that this has an equivalent training pathway to other practitioner routes which is evidently not the case. As such, it may be more appropriate to use terms such as "Cyberpsychology Practitioner", "Cyberpsychology Researcher" or similar when describing job roles.

One of the most important pieces of advice for cyberpsychology careers relates to the keywords and terms that are used when searching for job opportunities or exploring the range of options. "Cyberpsychology" is not a commonly used term in industry or by recruitment agencies when defining job roles. There will be cases where job roles relate directly to applying cyberpsychology, but these might be labelled as something else. Some alternative keywords which might be better to use within searches are:

- Human factors
- Behavioural science
- Science practitioner
- Behavioural insights

Of course, these terms might refer to roles which extend more broadly than cyberpsychology and online behaviour. Therefore, it is important to consider how these terms are being used based on the type of organisation these sit within, and the nature of a given job description. For example, if the job of a "Behavioural insights officer" is being advertised for a role in an online marketing company, then this is much more likely to relate to cyberpsychology than if it is being advertised for a job in a public health unit as part of a county council. As such, it is worth considering job roles and title in the context of the organisations they relate to. Table 3.1

Table 3.1 Examples of the types of sectors or organisations which might draw on cyberpsychology expertise

Type of company/sector	*Example companies*	*Indicative cyberpsychology insights*
Government agencies	e.g., MoD (Military of Defence), Home Office, DSTL (Defence Science & Technology Laboratory), Department of Homeland Security (DHS), Department of Defense (DoD), Environmental Protection Agency (EPA)	Human factors underpinning cyber threat, evidence to inform threat detection

(Continued)

Table 3.1 (Continued)

Type of company/sector	*Example companies*	*Indicative cyberpsychology insights*
Regional or local councils		Evidence to inform digital strategies or technology diffusion and innovation
Digital health and well-being tech companies		Evaluating digital tech products (i.e. do they actually encourage healthy lifestyle behaviours)
Communication services sector	Social technology or internet providers (e.g., Meta, Google)	Evaluating user experience, consumer insights etc.
Public sector	e.g., Academies, health councils (NHS), education services (DfE)	Evidence to inform policies and frameworks which feed into professional practice (e.g., gamification, technology-enhanced learning, digital tech, internet-mediated practice etc.)

gives some indicative examples of the types of sectors or organisations which might draw on cyberpsychology expertise and the types of ways the expertise is used.

In relation to more specific job titles relating to cyberpsychology, here are some indicative examples:

- Behavioural Scientist
- User Researcher
- Research Analyst
- UX/UCD Researcher
- Consumer Insights Officer
- Market Researcher
- Digital Marketing Coordinator/Officer
- Knowledge Manager
- Communications Officer

- Evidence Reviewer
- Patient Engagement Officer
- Evaluation Officer/Coordinator
- Project Officer/Coordinator
- (Digital) Wellness Officer
- Wellbeing Practitioner
- Policy and Evaluation Officer
- Cyber intelligence Officer

The context of the indicative job roles will be explored more specifically in the subsequent chapters which will make it more clear how these might relate to the types of knowledge in thematic areas of cyberpsychology, such as consumer cyberpsychology, health cyberpsychology, industrial-organisational cyberpsychology, and forensic and investigative cyberpsychology.

Becoming a consultant

As outlined earlier, oftentimes cyberpsychology expertise might be bought-in by companies who have specific digital challenges to overcome. In this case, there may be opportunities for those who are set up as consultants or business owners of cyberpsychology-related companies. As such, this section includes some general advice and practical considerations when settings oneself up as a consultant or founding a business, given this may be a fruitful option for many people seeking cyberpsychologically-informed careers.

Finding a common language

Adapting the language you use is one of the most fundamental considerations when knowing how to navigate the "lingo" of organisations, but so is knowing how to best communicate your own subject knowledge and insights to them.

As a starter, when selecting a suitable job title for your consultancy business, consider using terms which have been previously outlined in this chapter and which might be more familiar to businesses than the term "cyberpsychology". This might make more sense to organisations who might be interested in the types of insights you have who might otherwise be confused or put off by terms they may be unfamiliar with.

Table 3.2 Example industry terms and their academic equivalents

Industry/business terms	*Academic equivalent/example*
A/B testing	Testing effects between experimental conditions (e.g., stimulus A vs stimulus B on response, engagement rate, etc.)
Actionable insights	Applications of research/practical implications of research
Consumer insights	Participant perceptions or attitudes
Evidence review	Literature review
Onboarding (e.g., inducting new clients or employees into a company or in using a system)	Participant recruitment/sign-up; induction
Service evaluation	Intervention study
Slide-deck	Presentation slides
Value propositions	Key insights or value you have to offer (that you can put forward to help an organisation understand how you can help)
Work product	Assignment
Deliverable	Output
Benchmarking	Criteria

Another basic language principle, is to familiarise yourself with terms used by organisations, some of which might have equivalents in the academic world. Some examples are included in Table 3.2. In all cases, being familiar with what these refer to and adapting your own language to align to them can help establish some commonality in communication between you and client organisations, so you can help manage expectations and understanding.

In relation to technical language and understanding, it might also be helpful to up-skill yourself on this too. You do not necessarily need to be a highly skilled digital wizard, but to help align your communication with potential organisations and their challenges, it is worth having at least a basic understanding of things such as: how social media platforms work (e.g., algorithms, engagement loops), principles of user experience (UX) which might include how interfaces relate to user behaviour, AI components (chatbots, deepfakes, etc.), and fundamentals of cybersecurity (e.g., privacy, how risk is assessed/audited). This will help you better situate your insights in a relevant way, and that make sense to technical professionals or companies.

Transforming your communication

Whilst the above basic principles are important, there are more advanced communicational strategies to consider to best help organisations recognise how your subject knowledge can help them. Oftentimes this might simply be that you have to communicate how you can help them solve a challenge. This might involve the following steps:

1. Being aware of what sort of organisational challenges that type of organisation might typically face. It is often best to identify typical strategic challenges; the types of challenges that someone in the organisation's management or executive team might be most likely to care about. E.g., communications, training and development, performance management, productivity and efficiency, etc. Some examples of how you could communicate these might be that you can support organisations to:

    - improve the performance of products/services/processes which target consumer outcomes (e.g., by providing training or consultancy on the psychology of online communication to increase effectiveness of communications with consumers)
    - manage people and teams to support transformative organisational change (e.g., by providing training or consultancy on the psychology of motivation or behaviour change)
    - enhance strategic development or implementation (e.g., by providing consultancy to help them implement a new organisational digital strategy)

    In general, when communicating your subject knowledge, this is best pitched in the form of "actionable insights" rather than just a list of topics and your experience. Table 3.3 has some examples of how you can translate academic knowledge and

Table 3.3 Examples of actionable insights

Instead of...	*What insights do you have?*	*What are your actionable insights? (i.e. Why should they care?)*
I did a dissertation on the topic of visual processing of emoji. My results found significantly faster reaction times for those in the positive-valence condition compared to neutral ones.	My dissertation research identified that positive emotions depicted in emoji are useful for how we process information.	This might mean that using positive emoji in your brand's social media page could help consumers more easily understand the information you are giving them about your products
On my course, I did modules in personality psychology.	My course gave me the opportunity to learn about the psychology of individual differences. Particularly, personality traits are important for how likely we are to be persuaded by different types of messages.	This can be important to help us identify different personas in our company, so we can then personalise/tailor our company's internal email communications.
I have done extensive research on the topic of multimodal processing, and how we afford priority to visual stimuli over other sensory information. I have more than 50 publications in academic journals and am the editor of the journal *Cognitive Psychology*,	My research on processing helps me understand how we make sense of our physical world, and draw on different information from our senses.	My insights into sensory processing can help you understand how factors in our environment might affect work performance and productivity. I can help you evaluate how changes to your workplace environment might impact on employee performance data.

insights in this way. This helps you articulate your expertise in relation to how it aligns to the types of challenges they might be encountering, and therefore makes it easier for them to recognise how you can help them.

2 After identifying what your insights are, you next need to identify your *service offer*. This is how you will communicate and apply your subject knowledge when working with organisations. The type of services you provide might vary based on the types of expertise you have and how it aligns with the sorts of challenges organisations face. Some services might be more general (e.g., team training sessions) but others might need to be more bespoke based on how specifically the organisation feels they need to work with you on helping them solve their problem. Some examples of services include the following.

   - **Continued professional development (CPD) sessions or Learning and Development sessions** – these might be full or half day workshop type sessions in which you might deliver insights about your subject knowledge and offer some perspectives on its relevance to the organisation and the nature of its work. These might be designed to be general, or in other cases, might be more bespoke when the client organisation asks for something more specific or tailored. This is usually agreed at the point of drawing up a contract with them as something more tailored might have additional cost implications based on the additional preparation time needed.
   - **Consultancy** – this typically takes the form of advising or undertaking research work to a specified project. This would typically be bespoke to the client organisation and the deliverables (goals and outputs) would be agreed at the point of contract. This might consist of things like being interviewed to help the organisation ask targeted questions they need advice on, undertaking an evaluation to help the organisation assess how effective something is, or advising on how to design an evaluation of an initiative or campaign. These might be one-off or short-term contacts, but others might be longer-term pieces of work such as advising as a part of a change management programme over several months or years.

- **Lunch and Learn sessions** – these are typically one hour within a lunch break designed as enrichment to help the organisation's employees learn something new or consider new ideas

3 Finally, another consideration which relates to communication is about transforming your dissemination materials. That is, you might have some sort of dissertation, project portfolio or even academic papers relating to your subject knowledge that is relevant to your business offer. It is worth investing some time and effort in transforming these into more accessible materials. CEOs or management executives in organisations do not have the time or the incentive to read a 10,000 word dissertation or academic research paper. Therefore, consider writing lay summaries of your research, writing blog-posts, creating slide-decks (presentation slide summaries) or even developing some creative methods of communicating your subject knowledge (e.g., animations, comics, carousels etc.). These can all help communicate key insights in much more accessible and engaging ways.
4 From these more accessible artefacts, you then might need to drive traffic towards them. This is when well-designed email, SEO (search engine optimisation) and/or social media marketing strategies might be needed. Within this some things to consider will be:

- **Who is your target audience/market?** You will likely need to do some persona development, to identify specific characteristics of sub-groups of your target market based on things like their demographic, psychographic, geographic or behavioural characteristics. This can help you understand their likely motivations, needs and preferences, to help create more targeted messaging which aligns to these.
- **What platforms or channels might reach them best?** Based on your personas, you might have to stratify how you use different channels and methods of communication. Some subgroups might be more likely to occupy certain channels or platforms than others, so it is worth considering what might be prototypical environments for them.
- **Why might they be interested in my services?** This relates to the earlier point about how your insights correspond to likely organisational challenges or issues a company may be facing. Understanding why a company might be interested or what

might draw them to need your expertise, informs your messaging and how you "pitch" your expertise. This is likely to involve you considering what your unique selling point (USP) is relative to other similar services on the market, to help you recognise your competitive advantage. That is, why should they go to you for this service rather than someone else?

Practical considerations

In addition to the steps outlined above, there are also practical considerations to take forward to set yourself up effectively as a business owner.

1 Have a helpful website. This does not need to be overly comprehensive or too fancy. At the very least, it is useful having a couple of basic pages which cover things like: "About me"/"About [company name]" page, contact page, types of services, and research insights. This might extend to include more sophisticated content as you develop into your consulting role such as including example Case Studies, client testimonials, portfolios, etc. Additionally, consider how discoverable your website is from internet searches, and make use of useful keywords, and Search Engine Optimisation (SEO) features which some website service providers offer to aid visibility.
2 Up-skill yourself. There are many opportunities to up-skill yourself on developing your business, in respect of things like developing a business plan, marketing strategy, pricing plan, optimising social media marketing, financial management, and so on. For cyberpsychology-specific consultancy businesses, because these fall under the Digital Creative sector, it is worth exploring whether there are any business support programmes run by regional or local councils. These are typically funded by grant schemes such as the European Regional Development Fund, designed to support regional digital or creative business growth. Alternatively, LinkedIn Learning can be an excellent platform for sourcing training and development resources.
3 Get your business registered. In the UK, this is most likely with the HM Revenue & Customs. This will ensure that you are registered for corporation tax purposes. There are various considerations within this such as whether your business is a

sole trader, limited company or partnership, and what classification terms (Standard Industrial Classification (SIC) codes) best describe the nature of your business. As part of this, make sure you are familiar with processes such as self-assessment tax returns and similar.

4 Professional indemnity insurance. Having this type of insurance protects your business against claims made by your clients if they lose money because they followed your advice or due to negligent services they might claim you have offered. This can protect you in the case when legal fees, expenses, compensation costs, or other costs might be incurred in your defence of any claims.
5 Consider intellectual property protection. One example of this might be registering your trade mark (e.g., company name and/or logo) to protect your brand. In the UK, this can be done via the UK Government website.
6 Determine your pricing model and day rate as a consultant. There is not always straightforward as it depends on a lot of variables. As a general ball-park, in the UK, day rates can range between £500 and £5,000, averaging £1,500–£2,000. Some of the factors to consider in setting your pricing model include: your experience and expertise, your location, the type of client, your reputation, and what overhead costs you have (e.g., costs associated with renting office space, utility costs, insurance, marketing costs, any additional staffing costs, including bought-in services such as accounting or marketing specialists).

To summarise, I think it is fair to say that even though there are many roles that currently exist which can apply principles of cyberpsychology, these are not always "Cyberpsychologist" roles per se. Instead some effort is required in being creative in searching and communicating to ensure that relevant roles are realised. For anyone who is specifically seeking to have a job role which includes the term "cyberpsychology", the greatest opportunities here appear to be via business ownership/founding and consultancy rather than from roles that exist within organisations. Whilst it might be that things will change on this over time through increased recognition of cyberpsychology as a discipline, in the meantime, there are still plenty of ways to forge relevant career paths, albeit requiring a little more creative investment.

Resources

APA (American Psychological Association). (2022). *Careers in Applied Psychology: Human Factors Careers in Applied Psychology Panel.* Retrieved October 15, 2024, from https://youtu.be/V9PO1xzM7ws

BPS (British Psychological Society). Cyberpsychology Section (Careers tab) – https://www.bps.org.uk/member-networks/cyberpsychology-section

Gov.UK. Intellectual property and your work – https://www.gov.uk/intellectual-property-an-overview

Gov.UK. Set up a business – https://www.gov.uk/set-up-business

Medium. How much to charge as an independent consultant? Benchmarking consultancy fees based on sector and experience – https://medium.com/positive-momentum-partners/how-much-to-charge-as-an-independent-consultant-9843667ade96

Persona Builder. Marketing segmentation a complete guide to maximize your conversion rate – https://personabuilder.co/blog/marketing/marketing-segmentation-complete-guide

Smart Insights. The segmentation, targeting, positioning (STP) marketing model – https://www.smartinsights.com/digital-marketing-strategy/customer-segmentation-targeting/segmentation-targeting-and-positioning/

References

Cho, D., & Kwon, K.H. (2015). The impacts of identity verification and disclosure of social cues on flaming in online user comments. *Computers in Human Behavior, 51*, 363–372.

Folk, D., Heine, S.J., & Dunn, E. (2025). Individual differences in anthropomorphism help explain social connection to AI companions. *Scientific Reports 15*, 36548. https://doi.org/10.1038/s41598-025-19212-2

Kasneci, E., Sessler, K., Küchemann, S., et al. (2023). ChatGPT for good? On opportunities and challenges of large language models for education. *Learning and Individual Differences, 103*, 102274.

Kaye, L.K., Rousaki, A, Joyner, L.C., Barrett, L.A.F., & Orchard, L.J. (2022). The online behaviour taxonomy: A conceptual framework to understand behaviour in computer-mediated communication. *Computers in Human Behavior*, 107443. https://doi.org/10.1016/j.chb.2022.107443

Sproull, L., & Kiesler, S. (1986). Reducing social context cues: Electronic mail in organizational communication. *Management Science, 32*(11), 1492–1512.

Suler, J. (2004). The online disinhibition effect. *Cyberpsychology & Behavior, 7*(3), 321–326.

Wulff, D.U., & Mata, R. (2025). Semantic embeddings reveal and address taxonomic incommensurability in psychological measurement. *Nature Human Behaviour*, 1–11.

Chapter 4

Consumer cyberpsychology

Outline and definition of the theme

Consumer cyberpsychology relates to how digital or online environments shape consumer behaviour, and often has a primary goal of encouraging purchasing behaviour. Consumer psychology typically consists of understanding the psychological processes that influence how consumers engage with, and purchase products and services. This can include factors such as motivations (e.g., how needs might drive consumer behaviour), perceptions (e.g., how people process and engage with products, websites, how beliefs shape attitudes towards products or brands) and consumer decision-making, particularly in respect of purchasing behaviour (i.e. sales).

User experience (UX) can form a significant part of this, especially in the context of consumer behaviour occurring online, involving interactions with products and services via websites or software. A company's UX is a significant part of their brand's psychology: if the digital service (e.g., website) is clunky or not perceived to be easy to use, this can feed into user trust even if the product or service being sold might be faultless. In this way, poor UX can make or break consumer purchasing via perceptions relating to trust and satisfaction. Some of the principles of UX can equally apply to consumer psychology more widely. Some of these might include the impact of cognitive biases in consumer decision-making (albeit the cues which might prompt specific biases may have unique characteristics in online contexts), cognitive processes such as attention and cognitive load, heuristics, persuasive principles, and priming.

DOI: 10.4324/9781003581741-4

As well as UX, consumer marketing is another important aspect of consumer psychology. This can entail a broad range of activities which involve communicating with and selling to customers/consumers. The primary aim of consumer marketing is to understand what customers want and/or need, and develop messaging and experiences which align to these demands. Psychology as a discipline has always been useful in the context of consumer marketing, given that this can conceivably offer a window in the minds of consumers. On a general level, this can help understand what motivates people, and therefore can help marketers know how to optimise communication tactics and persuade people to engage with their brand and buy products or services.

However, in the context of digital or online marketing, this presents a multitude of new challenges which psychology, in its traditional sense, might not otherwise be able to address. The first of these is that behaviour can look different in online spaces compared to the offline world. Traditional psychological theories which explain and predict human behaviour therefore, might not be wholly sufficient for these rather specific or different digital behaviours. Relatedly, we might not fully understand how these online forms of behaviours correspond to user interests and characteristics. Therefore, we might need more specialised understanding from cyberpsychology of how online behaviour relates to user personality or other consumer characteristics. Secondly, we might not know what the optimal marketing behaviours and tactics are when in a digitalised format. That is, marketing tactics which work in offline contexts might not be easily translatable to online contexts. Third, the advancement of e-commerce and online marketing is increasing the rapidity of transactions, and therefore consumers and marketers might be engaging in behaviours sometimes in real-time. Finally, we need to recognise that the decision-making and constituent behaviours behind purchasing might intersect across both online and offline contexts, and therefore there is a need to recognise the interaction of these in the marketing funnel/consumer journey.

There are significant opportunities here for collaboration with cyberpsychology researchers. Regrettably, whilst marketers and brands themselves may have the ability to track a consumers' end-to-end journey, these behaviours remain largely unknown to psychologists. Additionally, the insights that cyberpsychology researchers might have about how online behaviours help us understand consumers often do not break through the boundaries of academic circles. As such cyberpsychology has a key role to play here to broker conversations which mean these different types of insights can be synergised to provide better understanding of consumers from their online behaviours.

Finally, measurements and methods in (cyber)psychology can present fruitful opportunities within consumer cyberpsychology contexts. For example, these may include understanding how to handle and analyse digital trace data and using eye-tracking for attention mapping on websites or other digital interfaces. Additionally, applying physiological and neurological measurements for exploring more in-depth emotional engagement and attention focus are key aspects of neuromarketing but equally could be fruitful when applying to digital interface design and interaction.

Prominent issues and topics

With respect of the literature underpinning consumer cyberpsychology, I briefly outline the major themes within this, and consider their relevance to cyberpsychology careers. These include: digital traces, perceptions from online behaviours, user motivations, user experience with different types of content, and persuasive communication.

What do digital traces reveal about user characteristics?

There is a wide literature on the topic of digital traces and their role within psychological science. This broadly explores the extent to which we can (accurately) identify individual differences such as demographics, personality, and attitudes through studying digital traces from people's interactions with technology. A large majority of this research has focused on personality traits, particularly the Big-5 traits (see Hinds & Joinson 2019). In respect of behaviours within social media platforms for example, research has found there to be distinguishable personality trait differences which are evident from certain digital behaviours. Such behaviours can include: user engagement with a given platform (Bowden-Green et al., 2020; Meng & Leung, 2021), "like" behaviour (Clark & Çallı, 2014; Kosinski et al., 2014), photo-sharing behaviour (Eftekhar et al., 2014), network size and number of group memberships (Kosinski et al., 2014), number of daily hours using Smartphone and message checks (Shaw, 2020), and behavioural engagement with video adverts (Yang & Zhao, 2021) Relatedly, digital traces which can be garnered from participation in e-WoM (electronic Word-of-Mouth) can be a means of understanding consumer loyalty (Cermak et al., 1994; Parrott et al., 2015; Wind & Rangaswamy, 2001; Woo Yoo et al. (2013), as well as being indicative of purchase intentions towards brand products or services.

From a consumer psychology perspective, these are clearly important insights. To be successful in consumer marketing and in shaping an effective user experience, it is paramount for brands/retailers to understand their markets, and how psychographic characteristics of users might help shape more segmented marketing tactics. As such, cyberpsychology evidence which maps how online behaviours relate to such user characteristics is clearly relevant and useful. However, there is an important balance to strike here: that is, over-personalisation can potentially back-fire when consumers may feel that an organisation knows them too well if this is too accurate. So the balance here is for these insights to be used to be assistive rather than as something more like surveillance.

Practical examples are presented in Case Studies 4 to 7 with Dr Georgia Crossland, Dr Lisa Orchard, Camila Caro and Roshelle Patterson all of whom have roles relating to analysing user experiences and behaviour. Georgia's research and data skills, alongside insight into user behaviour help inform how social media environments can be optimised for supporting effective user experiences. Similarly, Lisa, Camila and Roshelle's cyberpsychology subject knowledge and research skills enable them to critically apply insights to understanding user-centred behaviour and profiles.

Case study 4 Dr Georgia Crossland: User Experience (UX) Researcher at FAANG

Qualifications

- PhD in Psychology and Cyber Security

How Georgia applies cyberpsychology

- Leading strategic research within Risk and Privacy teams to enable the continuous development of privacy strategies and ensure user needs remain at the forefront of product development
- Using qualitative and quantitative methods (surveys, focus groups, field studies, usability tests, concept testing, ethnography, and one-on-one interviews) to develop product strategies and understand users

More information: https://www.bps.org.uk/blog/careers-cyberpsychology-conversation-dr-georgia-crossland

Case study 5 Dr Lisa Orchard: User Experience (UX) Researcher at a motoring retail company

Qualifications

- PhD in Psychology
- BSc (Hons) in Human Psychology

Networks

- Graduate Member of the British Psychological Society (BPS)

How Lisa applies cyberpsychology

- Applying cyberpsychological theory to interpret observations surrounding online shopping behaviours (e.g., Uses and Gratifications Theory allows for a consideration of why users may prefer certain shopping features

over others, or why a user may have a preference for a particular online retailer)
- Cyberpsychology can offer support for understanding the foundations of UX research (e.g., understanding processes of cognitive attention online can help shape suggestions of how online content should be developed)
- Using research skills to understand how to best measure online behaviours; for instance, how best to capture people's online shopping habits
- An awareness of AI and future developments in technology and their impacts is helpful for considering how these could be adopted within the organisation
- Understanding user-centric issues and measurements (which is commonplace in cyberpsychology) is helpful to advocate for the user and their needs from the technology

More information: https://ljorchard.wixsite.com/personal

Case study 6 Camila Caro: Customer Experience Analyst at Kaizen Gaming

Qualifications

- MSc in Cyberpsychology
- B.S. in Psychology

How Camila applies cyberpsychology

- Researching digital social behaviour to understand why users behave the way they do
- Using qualitative and quantitative methods (surveys, focus groups, interviews) for exploring user behaviour
- Using behavioural data to compare what users say they do with what they actually do online to get a more accurate user profile

- Measuring "digital empathy", studying the language used by chatbots, email and chat agents
- Quantifying "friendliness" in bots to understand how it impacts user trust and frustration

More information: https://www.linkedin.com/in/camilacaro04

Case study 7 Roshelle Patterson: Games UX Experience Researcher and Founder

Qualifications

- Masters in UX Design
- Bachelors in Psychology
- Associates in Intelligence Studies and Technology

Networks

- Ambassador for Women in Games
- IGDA Foundation

How Roshelle applies cyberpsychology

- Applying cyberpsychology to understand how players emotionally and cognitively engage with interactive systems, using rigorous UX research in games to map behaviour, perception, and decision-making inside complex digital worlds – turning player psychology into actionable design intelligence
- Bridging cyberpsychology with grief studies and death positivity, creating Playfully Mortal as a novel initiative that investigates how games can facilitate emotional processing, resilience, and community healing through

structured play, reflective practice, and evidence-based measurement.
- Operationalising cyberpsychology across the full ecosystem of players, developers, and communities, consulting on sensitive narrative design, building research-backed frameworks for emotionally responsible game design, and pioneering new models for play as a vehicle for care, empathy, and social good.

More information: https://www.linkedin.com/in/roshelleantoinette/

Newer advancements in consumer and marketing research have included the use of silicon samples (sometimes referred to as synthetic datasets). These are generated based on large language models which replicate respondents' behaviour. Within a consumer context, this might include generating silicon samples which mirror the characteristics of specific consumer groups based on key psychographic or demographic characteristics and asking these samples to respond to tasks in a way which would mirror how humans with these characteristics would do. Essentially, this can help companies predict how certain types of marketing content or input might be responded to by different personas. Researchers have started to use this approach in academic research (Argyle et al., 2023; Demszky et al., 2023; Dillion et al., 2023). Some studies have shown that this approach may have a value in replicating human responses given that similar biases that exist in humans also apply to silicon samples (Binz & Schulz, 2023). However, other research suggests there to be significant differences between samples (Kirshner, 2024), highlighting silicon samples perhaps not yet being suitable replacements for human participants.

Scholars have outlined some of the challenges and opportunities regarding use of silicon samples and have identified the conditions under which these might be considered most efficacious in respect of the nature of tasks and settings (Sarstedt et al., 2024). A particular opportunity in consumer and marketing contexts relates to them being used as part of pre-testing or piloting, as a way of identifying potential errors or measurement scale issues prior to human testing (Sarstedt et al., 2024). As such, this is a promising use of AI within a consumer setting, and highlights the value of cyberpsychology insight into these types of professional domains.

Perceptions based on online behaviour

Another prominent literature-base which is informative for consumer cyberpsychology is that of perceptions associated with online behaviour. Broadly this is concerned with how corporate visual identity (CVI) or other identity markers of brands impact on perceptions such as reputation, credibility and trustworthiness. Research in this domain for example has studied the effectiveness of different online behaviours as identity cues (Akström & Sveningsson, 2019; DeAndrea et al., 2010; Zhao et al., 2008), and how these might relate to consumer perceptions and subsequent behaviour (Bakshy et al., 2012; Bapna & Umyarov, 2015; Taylor et al., 2022; Tucker, 2016).

The Brands as Intentional Agents Framework (BIAF; Kervyn et al., 2022), which derives from the more general Stereotype Content Model (SCM; Fiske et al., 2002) outlines that consumers' perceptions tend to fit into two dimensions of warmth (intentions) and competence (ability). Psychology has widely acknowledged these two dimensions as being relevant to our perceptions and tendencies towards social groups. In the case of the BIAF, this has been widely applied to understanding how consumers form perceptions of brands (Bennett et al., 2013; Kervyn et al., 2022; Zawisza & Pittard, 2015). Arguably, perceptions of warmth align to characteristics about trustworthiness or friendliness, and competence more towards ability or initiative. Research suggests that associated perceptions of warmth and admiration have strong effects on consumers' attitudes and purpose intentions with brands (Ivens et al., 2015). Additionally, other research suggests that brand personality can be characterised via five dimensions of sophistication, sincerity, competence, ruggedness, and excitement (Aaker, 1997), and perceptions of these can in turn be antecedents to warmth and competence perceptions (Aaker, 1997).

In respect of applied implications, there is clearly merit for brands understanding how different cues or behaviours relate to their user/consumers' perceptions, particularly as perceptions feed directly into brand reputation. In online consumer contexts, there is a key role for applying cyberpsychology evidence when exploring how online cues and behaviours may function in this respect. This is especially relevant when behaviours might be somewhat distinct relative to offline consumer contexts. A specific example of uniqueness relates to the use of AI within consumer contexts. That is, when AI is used in activities such as content generation (written and image-based), and as AI-assistance in the form of chat bots to support customer service, there are key concerns here about user experience. As noted in Case Study 6, Camila's role includes understanding language used by chatbots and agents, and quantifying how best to measure "friendliness" of these to consider impacts such as consumer trust. Clearly, understanding user attitudes, perceptions and impacts associated with different types of AI content and engagement is a pertinent issue and presents a strong case for how cyberpsychological insights might be especially relevant here.

Another value that cyberpsychology can bring to the issue of perceptions and online behaviours is that consumer behaviour with brands often operates within communities, not just with the brand itself. As such, the way people curate aspects of their identity in respect of online brand interactions often takes place within an associated community (e.g., a brand or company's social media site). As such, consumers are community-builders or contributors not just audiences. Therefore, it is important that brands or companies take forward insights from cyberpsychology on topics such as online communities and interactions, to know how these communities might be built and nurtured to best support brand reputation.

User motivations and behaviours

Within consumer-based contexts, understanding user motivations particularly around purchasing behaviour is clearly relevant. Whilst the field of consumer psychology can present a wide array of valuable theoretical insights into user motivation and behaviour, there are perhaps some specific nuances to consider in respect of online-based consumer contexts.

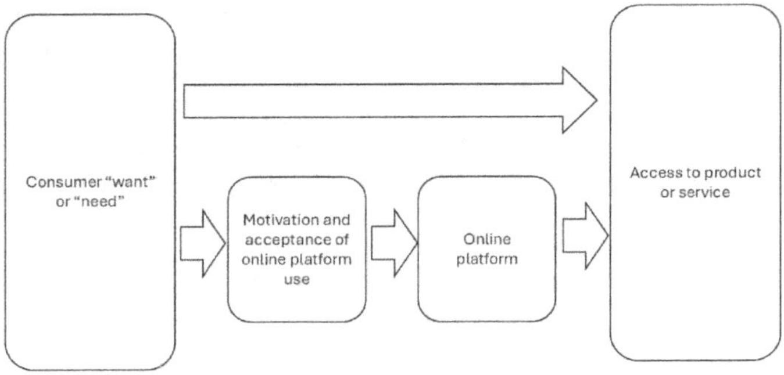

Figure 4.1 Consumer motivation in online versus offline contexts

In respect of user motivation with technology, this essentially seeks to understand the "why"; that is, why do people want or need to use a given platform and its features? This adds an additional level into the consumer motivation and purchasing behaviour process, given that user motivation and acceptance of specific online platforms could arguably form a barrier to access and purchasing of products or services. Figure 4.1. illustrates how online platform motivation and access might differ from offline consumer purchasing flows. As such, it is important to understand motivations in respect of the digital aspect of consumer behaviour when this occurs within online consumer contexts.

A central aspect of user motivation can be boiled down to "why": that is, why will this specific platform be useful for fulfilling my need or want? There can be various theoretical perspectives from cyberpsychology which are relevant to understand this. These include: Uses and Gratifications Theory (Blumler & Katz, 1974; LaRose & Eastin, 2004; LaRose et al., 2001), Mood Management Theory (Zillmann, 1988a, 1988b; Zillman & Bryant, 1985), and theories relating to technology acceptance (Davis et al., 1989; Marangunić & Granić, 2015; Venkatesh et al., 2012)

Starting with Uses and Gratifications Theory, this posits that there are trait-like psychological needs or perceptions which drive media use and engagement. These motivations are: need for identity, diversion/escapism, relationships/social, and surveillance. These drive the specific media sought and in instances where the need or want is gratified, this explains continued use. Recent work has applied Uses and Gratifications Theory to understand smartphone use (Hiniker et al., 2016). Within this, the authors draw distinctions between "instrumental" and "ritualistic" purposes of using smartphones. Instrumental uses are those which are goal-directed and purposeful whereas the latter are those which are habitual. Other research applying these principles has found that underlying motivations play a key role in determining the usage and behaviours associated with the technological activity (Hilvert-Bruce et al., 2018). For example, the extent to which users' motivations for social media live-streaming are gratified by the platform, determines usage behaviour such as time spent engaging in live-streaming. As such, it is clearly important to account for technologically orientated motivations given they can largely determine how consumers interact and engage with products and services.

Other theoretical ideas include Mood Management Theory (Zillmann, 1988a), which outlines how mood state drives selective consumption and exposure in relation to media. Unlike Uses and Gratifications Theory, Mood Management Theory is more state-like, suggesting that these needs or wants broadly vary within people and over time and contexts. In respect of consumer contexts, this suggests that integrating expressions of valence into online platforms and marketing messages might be important to consider to accommodate the way that selection of services and products might be mood-driven. There are also implications for user research and market insights. Namely, if user psychographic profiles, such as their needs and motivations, do not stay static over time, this raises questions about the validity of one-time measurements and capture of user personas. This clearly indicates that fluidity is needed with respect to user insight measurement given the potential dynamic nature of user needs and motivations across time and context.

Finally, other theoretical explanations around user motivations relate to technology acceptance. Perspectives such as those in Technology Acceptance Model (Davis et al., 1989; Marangunić & Granić, 2015), Unified Theory of Acceptance and Use of Technology (Venkatesh et al., 2012), and Technology Integration Model (Shaw et al., 2018) explain how perceptions about technology relate to acceptance and therefore (continued) use. User perceptions include: ease of use, and usefulness, as well as those relating to contextual variables, such as facilitating conditions and social factors. These theoretical principles are useful for helping establish the barriers and enablers associated with uptake of specific digital or online platforms, and therefore identify how to optimise user adoption via effective usability and user experience processes. However, within consumer contexts, particularly when product or service engagement and purchasing is heavily reliant on online platforms, there are potential risks to sales in cases where poor usability exists, impacting upon user perceptions and experiences of use. These theoretical models can inform how best to measure user attitudes and perceptions of a given platform, which can be helpful to integrate into usability testing of platforms alongside the usual more technical aspects of the process.

Following on from considering user motivation, it is equally important to have a user-centric perspective of user behaviour and interactions when considering online consumer environments. When considering this in the context of social media, understanding individual differences in behavioural styles of social media use can be insightful given this might signal the extent to which people engage actively in consumer content on social platforms. Research has identified that there are distinct behavioural styles of social media use such as interactive, reactive, and passive use (Shaw et al., 2022; Pennington et al., 2025), and that there can be a wide array of constituent behaviours which sit under these (Kaye et al., 2024). Some users might simply consume content (passive use) whereas others might respond to others' content (reactive use) or engage fully in it (interactive use). In the context of consumer behaviour, these could represent different profiles of user, which might signal where different strategies are needed to encourage consumer engagement via social marketing. Additionally, research suggests there to be key traits such as empathetic concern and social motivation which seem to relate more to users who are more interactive in their social media behaviours relative to passive users (Pennington et al., 2025). As such, there seems to be some indication that understanding user traits relating to social and interpersonal tendencies can be informative for signalling user characteristics, and therefore helps predict online behavioural styles.

Taken together, insights from cyberpsychology can provide helpful frameworks for knowing how best to measure user motivations and behavioural tendencies which can be informative to how consumer market research or insight research might be best conducted. This can present opportunities for enhancing evidence-informed methods for measuring and understand consumers.

User experiences with types of content/messages

Within digital environments, content can refer to many different things. The format of this can range from being text, audio, audio-visual or a combination of these. Cyberpsychology underpins the user experience of how we engage and process different formats of content, especially when we consider these as a part of mediated communication such as online marketing or consumer interactions.

There are various theoretical models which explain how types of media content and messages might have differential impacts on user experiences and the potential effectiveness of mediated communication. These are broadly situated within Social Information Processing Theory (Walther, 1992) which explains the way we obtain social information to help support interpersonal processes. Particularly online, it is noted that we might often overcompensate for the typical absence of non-verbal cues (Walther, 1996). This is particularly likely when the media or format we are interacting via is less "rich" in nature. There are various theories within cyberpsychology which can explain how richness of media is related to different user experiences. These theories are discussed below.

Media Richness Theory (Daft & Lengel, 1986) posits that the receiver's processing or understanding of a message is influenced primarily by the richness of the way it is presented (Daft & Lengel, 1986). Messages which can extend the perceptual bandwidth such as via multimodal communication (e.g., concurrent visual and audio modalities) are said to be higher in richness than communications which might be unimodal or text-based (Wang et al., 2023). Four key factors are said to determine the level of media richness: i) number of cues being used to convey a message; ii) number of meanings which can be expressed through symbols used; iii) how quickly responses can be issued; and iv) level of personalisation within the message (Daft et al., 1987).

Similarly, Media Naturalness Theory (Kock, 2005, 2011) builds on the aforementioned principles. A key distinction here, however, is that this refers to the extent to which the behaviour encompassed within a message aligns to what is considered to meet natural communication characteristics. Here, behaviour which mirrors face-to-face communication would be argued to be the "gold standard" of natural communication relative to other derivates of communication, such as text-based exchanges. This focuses on five elements of i) high levels of co-location, ii) synchronicity, ability to express and observe facial expressions, iv) express and observe body language, and v) express and listen to speech.

The focus in Media Naturalness Theory is on behaviour itself which exists within the message exchange rather than the richness of the platform or channel by which this behaviour is being communicated. Arguably, media richness and naturalness tend to be strongly associated, but there can be instances in which the underpinning behaviour is represented distinctly within a computer-mediated communicative exchange (Kaye et al., 2022). The consequences of this are said to have differential effects, whereby less natural behaviour draws upon greater cognitive resources, and this can bring on additional cognitive load within processing (Kock, 2004).

Extending further from the aforementioned theories, Channel Expansion Theory (Carlson & Zmud, 1999) emphasises the role of the receiver and their perceptions of media richness. More specifically, this posits that through experience/expertise with a communication platform, users acquire and enrich their capabilities and perceptual affordances of it (D'Urso, 2020). That is, the more experience a user has with using a specific channel or platform of communication, the richer they perceive it to be. Four elements are discussed as being relevant here: i) experience with the channel, ii) experience with the message topic, iii) experience with the context, and iv) experience with the communication partner. Essentially, this theory recognises the interaction of social and cognitive elements of processing which might be relevant to understand the receiver processing of online messages.

One of the key distinctions of online marketing relative to more traditional broadcasting marketing and advertising is its interactive and dynamic nature. This relates to the interactive nature of the functions and features of online environments which affect marketers' and consumers' experiences and engagement with marketing content. Interactivity can relate to the modality of content (text, audio, visual), source/platform or the message itself (Sundar, 2007). In relation to modality of content, marketing content can be represented in many ways and, particularly with regards to social media, in many cases may be multimodal in nature (e.g., text or captions with visual images or videos). Much research has been done on the topic of interactivity. Broadly, this has found that greater interactivity relates positively to user attitudes (Sundar, 1998; Sundar, 2000). This has been found in relation to both modality interactivity and source interactivity (such as greater customisation ability) (Kalyanaraman & Sundar, 2006). Additionally, message contingency which is demonstrated through responsiveness and interactivity across a series of messages, has been found to be appraised more positively where there are higher levels of interactivity between them (Rafaeli, 1988; Sundar et al., 2003).

There are clearly some useful evidence-informed insights which can be taken from this which apply to the way that brands or retailers might make use of different types of interactive content or functions within their online platforms, including websites and any accompanying social channels, which enhance user/consumer attitudes and behaviours relating to their products, services or indeed their brand itself.

Taking this further, the use of Virtual Reality (VR) is an attractive option for brands or retailers to understand more about consumer shopping or browsing experiences. This might relate to physical consumer behaviour, but making use of the digital to better measure the navigational and decision-making processes to the consumer journey. There are interesting cyberpsychology-related frameworks that are relevant here including Social Presence Theory (Short et al., 1976), and other principles relating to embodiment. Essentially, principles from these frameworks are relevant to understanding how enhanced embodiment or perceived sense of presence in an environment or with others, enhances immersion, positive experiences, and also proffers a suitable simulated environment for user testing.

As a practical example relating to consumer cyberpsychology, Case Study 8 introduces Dr Rachel Kowert who is a founder of a company which produces multimedia content regarding cyberpsychology education for the general public. Insights regarding how to develop engaging and interactive content underpin the success of her business.

Case study 8 Dr Rachel Kowert: Founder at Psychgeist

Qualifications

- PhD in Psychology
- MA in Counselling Psychology
- BA in Psychology

Networks

- Digital Games Research Association (DiGRA)
- International Communication Association (ICA)

How Rachel applies cyberpsychology

- Producing multimedia content for the science of games and pop culture to help reach public and practitioner awareness of the scientific evidence regarding popular media
- Product and policy advising for a range of game and game adjacent organisations, such as, Discord, Ubisoft, Sony, and Microsoft

More information: www.rkowert.com

Persuasive communication

Another key theme in the academic literature relates to persuasive communication. This is often in relation to understanding how to use principles of persuasion to encourage consumer purchasing and also how these feed into personalisation and behavioural targeting.

There is a wide literature base which has studied the applications of models of persuasion such as the Elaboration Likelihood Model (ELM; Petty & Cacioppo, 1986) to the marketing context (Leong et al., 2019; Li, 2013; Liao & Huang, 2021;

Zheng et al., 2022). The ELM outlines central versus peripheral routes of processing, which may each result in persuasive effects (Handley & Runnion, 2011). The central route refers to conscious or careful consideration of content. However, people may not always be able or motivated to process the entirety of message content via this central route and instead process via the peripheral route. This alternative route typically is dependent upon heuristic cues such as one's attitudes towards the message source (e.g., the person disseminating the message) and is considered a more superficial level of processing.

Previous research which has applied the ELM has identified that central factors such as information quality, perceived credibility, accuracy, and usefulness of content all have the potential to influence consumer attitudes towards beauty products (Wang & Lee, 2019; Weismueller et al., 2020). However, peripheral factors have also been noted to be relevant. For example, source trustworthiness, perceived expertise and attractiveness of influencers (Wang & Lee, 2019), linguistic style of posts (Lee & Theokary, 2021), source credibility (Li, 2013; Taylor et al., 2022; Teng et al., 2014), and perceived parasocial relationships with the messenger (Masuda et al., 2022) have all been found to be related to user attitudes and in some cases, subsequent online behaviours.

Other relevant psychological models which can be applied to online marketing and communication include behaviour change models such as the Theory of Planned Behaviour (Ajzen, 1991), Theory of Reasoned Action (Fishbein & Ajzen, 1975) or COM-B model (Michie et al., 2011). Indeed, the COM-B model incorporates communication/marketing as one of the intervention functions which frames how the different sources of behaviour change might be aligned. Specifically, the component of motivation (reflective and automatic) is noted as a key source which might be targeted via marketing/communication functions to encourage behaviour change.

Whilst the COM-B is more typically applied to health psychology, there are clear applications more widely, including online consumer marketing and impacts on encouraging purchasing behaviour. However, to date, there are only a handful of empirical studies which have applied this model in this context. For example, research has applied this model to understand how to motivate online consumers to interact and build trust with online experts to encourage purchasing behaviour via expert recommendations (Li & Kang, 2022). Other research has applied it to explore how beauty app users' perceptions of motivation and opportunity relate to their behaviours of using a beauty industry matchmaking platform (Chang & Hsu, 2022). Despite its value as a theoretical basis for understanding how to encourage or change consumers' online behaviour, there is scant evidence available in the academic literature in this regard. As such, there are a wide range of opportunities here for (cyber)psychology principles to be used more constructively in online consumer marketing contexts. However, perhaps more recent advancements in AI-enabled advertising and communication methods (e.g., AI assistants) perhaps highlight the need to understand the way these intersect with consumer behaviour in online environments, and their role in potentially changing consumers' motivations and attitudes towards products and services, and the impact of these on purchasing behaviours.

Other theoretical principles include persuasive principles outlined by Cialdini (2001). These include, scarcity, social proof, reciprocity, authority, liking, and commitment. The authority principle relates to the notion that people are inclined to follow messages from a person in authority (Blass, 1991). Consensus or social proof relates to how people observe others to inform their behaviour (e.g., often prompted by use of reviews, testimonials, ratings etc.). The principle of commitment refers to the way people undertake a behaviour which is aligned with their previous behaviour or is consistent with their beliefs. Scarcity relates to people's perceptions about the value or uniqueness of a product or service (e.g., "only two left!"). Liking refers to the observation that people are more likely to endorse attitudes or behaviours towards people they like. Finally, reciprocity refers to the inclination to return a favour to others (e.g., free trials, useful content). As such, when used ethically, these nudges can increase conversion. It is important however, to balance this carefully, as if these are observed to be used in an obvious and manipulative way, they can easily compromise long-term consumer trust.

Within online consumer contexts, there may be cues which exist in these environments which might be unique compared to offline consumer psychology, and so some cyberpsychological insight can be helpful to understand how these might apply and the potential impact on consumer behaviour. For example, in respect of social proof/consensus principles, within online consumer marketing, there can be cues such as social media "likes" or shares and so on posts, or on websites, pop-ups with messages such as "12 other people are looking at this" or similar might signal social proof within online contexts. In the context of influencer marketing, it is quite easy to see how some of these principles might be applied, such as "liking" which could be a mechanism by which influencers with high appeal and relatability might be highly effective in persuading online brand purchasing.

Another realm which relates to persuasion online is influencers. That is, these are individuals with large social media followings who operate on behalf of companies to sell their products or services. Whilst the academic literature on influencers is very much evolving, there are key principles from (cyber)psychology which apply when understanding the effectiveness of influencers. These may include principles relating to parasocial relationships, social comparison, and how characteristics and cues such as authenticity relate to user trust of these individuals (Bi & Zhang, 2023; Conde & Casais, 2023). Enhancing users' perceptions of trust and credibility via strengthening perceptions of parasocial relationships with these individuals, and enhancing users' desire to be more like them, are all relevant psychological principles for effective persuasion.

As practical examples relating to consumer cyberpsychology, Case Studies 9 and 10 introduce contrasting example cases of consultants who focus on consumer-related issues. Dr Paul Marsden helps businesses understand how digital advances affect users' motivation, expectations, and behaviour, whereas Alan Gray is focused more on supporting businesses to build effective connection and communication with consumers.

Case study 9 Dr Paul Marsden: Consumer Psychologist at Syzygy and Brand Genetics

Qualifications

- PhD in Psychology
- MSc in Psychology of Fashion

Networks

- Chartered Psychologist with the British Psychological Society (BPS)

How Paul applies cyberpsychology

- Helping businesses and brands make sense of these shifts and help them adapt to the ways tech is changing our lives, work, and relationships
- Consulting on the psychology of online behaviour – why and how – people buy
- Researching on how AI and emerging digital technologies change motivations, expectations and behaviours
- Developing in-house virtual AI co-worker "Lexi" – an AI psychoanalyst who does AI QDA (qualitative data analysis)
- Writing blog-posts/articles on the topic of digital well-being to help inform public and businesses

More information: https://www.youtube.com/watch?reload=9&v=go5SIf56EpY&feature=youtu.be

Case study 10 Alan Gray: Freelance cyberpsychology Consultant and Founder of GrayArea

Qualifications

- MSc

Networks

- Chartered Psychologist and Associate Fellow with the British Psychological Society

How Alan applies cyberpsychology

- Providing a psychological consultation service for small businesses particularly around using behavioural science to connect with audiences and optimise communications
- Delivering workshops and training for small businesses on topics such as influence, persuasion, relationships, and connection
- Using behavioural insights to inform product development and enhance consumer behaviour and satisfaction
- Writing articles, blogs, and whitepapers

More information: https://www.bps.org.uk/blog/careers-cyberpsychology-conversation-alan-gray

Summary of key impacts of cyberpsychology

Here is a summary of the key impacts from these key themes in the research literature and Case Studies.

- **Digital traces** – cyberpsychology insights can offer a scientifically informed user-centred perspective. This applies strongly to practical areas such as online consumer insights and user research. This can help marketing be more targeted and personalised to different consumer groups (i.e. personas). For example, in market segmentation, establishing the various personas of one's consumer-base in relation to demographic, psychographic or behavioural characteristics is designed to address this type of targeted marketing. However, the rigour regarding how these personas are identified is perhaps less established and therefore offers an opportunity for cyberpsychological insights
- **Perceptions from online behaviours** – cyberpsychology insights can be informative to organisations or brands about how they might express their corporate or brand identity in a way that is perceived as favourable, reputable, and congruent to their brand values and messaging. Additionally, in the context of AI

within consumer contexts, it is relevant to consider user attitudes, perceptions, and impacts associated with this
- **Understanding user motivations and behaviours** – cyberpsychology insights can provide a more user-centric perspective to how user needs can be accommodated and how this impacts upon how user characteristics are measured within online consumer environments
- **Impacts of interactivity** – cyberpsychology insights are informative towards understanding the impact of interactive and dynamic features within online marketing sources or environments. This can be informative about ensuring optimal levels of interactivity in materials and in developing effective processes of online community management between consumers and brands/organisations
- **Persuasive communication** – cyberpsychology insights can be informative about the level of processing being afforded to various marketing sources to help determine what might be most optimal in driving consumer attitudes and behaviour

Advice

As outlined in Chapter 3, ensuring you are translating your insights into language that makes sense to your target clients is paramount to be able to successfully engage as a cyberpsychology consultant. In the case of consumer cyberpsychology, the types of clients are likely to be retail, brands, product developers, digital marketers, and social technology companies. Some indicative examples of types of insights that relate to these include the following.

- Commercial or retail sector: e.g., working with brands to support their digital marketing strategy, or communicate their brand identity
- Communication services sector: e.g., working with social technology providers or brands in things like prototype/product development and testing, analysing user data and behaviour, and user insights analysis.
- Marketing sector: e.g., market research, social media marketing, brand management, advertising, and digital marketing

Although having qualifications or experience in subjects such as Marketing and Communications will be really helpful, there are key areas which are worth doing some self-study on, to better understand the types of things that organisations will be interested in. Some of these might include the following.

- Marketing/Sales funnel – the journey that consumers take from initial awareness of a product or service, to purchasing it
- Brand awareness – ensuring people are aware of the brand, its purpose and key messages
- Brand reputation – ensuring a brand is considered reputable in the eyes of consumers and the sector
- Data-driven insights – ensuring that any decisions regarding products/services are informed by user/consumer data and patterns/trends
- Optimising user experience – making changes to a digital system or product to ensure there is a seamless interaction between users and the digital interface and the channels surrounding it
- Targeted campaigns/target audiences – designing communications in a way which is personalised based on characteristics of users/consumers such as demographics, psychographics, geography etc.
- Brand community – a collection of users/consumers who form a community in support or advocacy of a brand and its products/services
- Pay-per-click advertising (PPC) – a digital marketing strategy where advertisers pay a fee each time a user clicks on their online advert
- SEO (Search Engine Optimization) marketing – a process to improve visibility of websites and their content, in search engine results pages such as on Google results

Indicative keywords and job roles

- Online consumer insights
- Online market insights
- Online data insights
- Digital marketing/online marketing

- User research
- User experience (UX)
- User-centred design (UCD)
- Human-computer interaction (HCI)
- E-commerce
- Customer systems and analytics
- Customer/consumer experience
- User Researcher
- UX/UCD Researcher
- Consumer Insights Officer
- Market Researcher
- Digital Marketing Coordinator/Officer
- Knowledge Manager
- Communications Officer
- Research Analyst
- Product Developer
- Product Analyst

Resources

Fox-Hamilton, N. (2024). Consumer cyberpsychology and online marketing. In G. Kirwan, I. Connolly, H. Barton & M. Palmer (Eds), *An Introduction to Cyberpsychology*. Routledge.

Kaye, L.K., & Joyner, L.C. (2025). Cyberpsychology and Digital Marketing: The new frontier for effective social media marketing? In M. Wright (Ed.), *Research Handbook on Cyberpsychology*. Edward Elgar Publishing.

Ramsey, P. (2025). *Psychology UX Glossary*. Retrieved October 16, 2025, from https://builtformars.com/ux-glossary

The Decision Lab (2025). *Consumer Psychology* – https://thedecisionlab.com/reference-guide/psychology/consumer-psychology

UX Psychology Newsletter by Dr Maria Panagiotidi – https://uxpsychology.substack.com/

Yablonski, J. (2025). *Laws of UX*. Retrieved October 16, 2025, from https://lawsofux.com/

References

Aaker, J.L. (1997). Dimensions of brand personality. *Journal of Marketing Research, 34*(3), 347. https://doi.org/10.2307/3151897

Ajzen, I. (1991). The theory of planned behavior. *Organizational Behavior and Human Decision Processes, 50*(2), 179–211. https:/doi.org.10.1016/0749-5978(91)90020-T

Akström, M., & Sveningsson, M. (2019). Young people's experiences of political membership: From political parties to Facebook groups. *Information, Communication & Society, 22*(2), 155–171. https://doi.org/10.1080/1369118X.2017.1358294

Argyle, L.P., Busby, E.C., Fulda, N., Gubler, J.R., Rytting, C., & Wingate, D. (2023). Out of one, many: Using language models to simulate human samples. *Political Analysis, 31*(3), 337–351. https://doi.org/10.1017/pan.2023.2

Bakshy, E., Rosenn, I., Marlow, C., & Adamic, L. (2012). The role of social networks in information diffusion. In *Proceedings of 21st International Conference on World Wide Web*, 519–528. ACM.

Bapna, R., & Umyarov, A. (2015). Do your online friends make you pay? A randomized field experiment on peer influence in online social networks. *Management Science, 61*, 1902–1920

Bennett, A.M., Hill, R.P., & Oleksiuk, D. (2013). The impact of disparate levels of marketplace inclusion on consumer–brand relationships. *Journal of Public Policy & Marketing, 32*(1), 16–31. https://doi.org/10.1509/jppm.12.023

Bi, N.C., & Zhang, R. (2023). "I will buy what my 'friend' recommends": The effects of parasocial relationships, influencer credibility and self-esteem on purchase intentions. *Journal of Research in Interactive Marketing, 17*(2), 157–175. https://doi.org/10.1108/JRIM-08-2021-0214

Binz, M., & Schulz, E. (2023). Using cognitive psychology to understand GPT-3. *Proceedings of the National Academy of Sciences, 120*(6), e2218523120. https://doi.org/10.1073/pnas.2218523120

Blass, T. (1991). Understanding behavior in the Milgram obedience experiment: The role of personality, situations, and their interactions. *Journal of Personality and Social Psychology, 60*(3), 398. https://doi.org/10.1037/0022-3514.60.3.398

Blumler, J.G., & Katz, E. (1974). The uses of mass communications: Current perspectives on gratifications research. *Sage Annual Reviews of Communication Research, 3*.

Bowden-Green, T., Hinds, J., & Joinson, A. (2020). How is extraversion related to social media use? A literature review. *Personality and Individual Differences, 164*, 110040. https://doi.org/10.1016/j.paid.2020.110040

Carlson, J.R., & Zmud, R.W. (1999). Channel expansion theory and the experiential nature of media richness perceptions. *Academy of Management Journal, 42*(2), 153–170. https://doi.org/10.2307/257090

Cermak, D.S.P., File, K.M.K., & Prince, P.A. (1994). Customer participation in service specification and delivery. *Journal of Applied Business Research, 10*(2), 90–98.

Chang, Y-W., & Hsu, Y. (2022). The factors that affect members' use of a beauty industry matchmaking platform: Validation of the COM-B extended model. *Frontiers in Psychology*, 13. https://doi.org/10.3389/fpsyg.2022.976109

Cialdini, R.B. (2001). The science of persuasion. *Scientific American, 284*(2), 76–81.

Clark, L., & Çallı, L. (2014). Personality types and Facebook advertising: An exploratory study. *Journal of Direct, Data and Digital Marketing Practice, 15*(4), 327–336. https://doi.org/10.1057/dddmp.2014.25

Conde, R., & Casais, B. (2023). Micro, macro and mega-influencers on Instagram: The power of persuasion via the parasocial relationship. *Journal of Business Research, 158,* 113708. https://doi.org/10.1016/j.jbusres.2023.113708

Daft, R.L., & Lengel, R.H. (1986). Organizational information requirements, media richness and structural design. *Management Science, 32*(5), 554–571. https://doi.org/10.1287/mnsc.32.5.554

Daft, R.L., Lengel, R.H., & Trevino, L.K. (1987). Message equivocality, media selection, and manager performance: Implications for information systems. *MIS Quarterly, 11*(3), 355–366. https://doi.org/10.2307/248682

Davis, F.D., Bagazzie, R.P., & Warshaw, P.R. (1989). User acceptance of computer technology: A comparison of two theoretical model authors. *INFORMS, 35*(8), 982–1003.

DeAndrea, D.C., Shaw, A.S., & Levine, T.R. (2010). Online language: The role of culture in self-expression and self-construal on Facebook. *Journal of Language and Social Psychology, 29*(4), 425–442. https://doi.org/10.1177/0261927X10377989

Demszky, D., Yang, D., Yeager, D.S., Bryan, C.J., Clapper, M., Chandhok, S., Eichstaedt, J. C., Hecht, C., Jamieson, J., Johnson, M., Jones, M., Krettek-Cobb, D., Lai, L., Mitchell, N.J., Ong, D.C., Dweck, C.S., Gross, J.J., & Pennebaker, J.W. (2023). Using large language models in psychology. *Nature Reviews Psychology, 2,* 688–701. https://doi.org/10.1038/s44159-023-00241-5

Dillion, D., Tandon, N., Gu, Y., & Gray, K. (2023). Can AI language models replace human participants? *Trends in Cognitive Sciences, 27*(7), 597–600. https://doi.org/10.1016/j.tics.2023.04.008

D'Urso, S.C. (2020). Channel Expansion Theory. In J. Bulck (Ed.), *The International Encyclopedia of Media Psychology* (1st ed., pp. 1–6). Wiley. https://doi.org/10.1002/9781119011071.iemp0119

Eftekhar, A., Fullwood, C., & Morris, N. (2014). Capturing personality from Facebook photo and photo-related activities: How much exposure do you need? *Computers in Human Behavior, 37,* 162–170.

Fishbein, M., & Ajzen, I. (1975). Predicting and understanding consumer behavior: Attitude-behavior correspondence. In I. Ajzen & M. Fishbein (Eds), *Understanding Attitudes and Predicting Social Behavior* (pp. 148–172). Englewood Cliffs, NJ: Prentice Hall.

Fiske, S.T., Cuddy, A.J.C., Glick, P., & Xu, J. (2002). A model of (often mixed) stereotype content: Competence and warmth respectively follow from perceived status and competition. *Journal of Personality and Social Psychology, 82*(6), 878–902. https://doi.org/10.1037/0022-3514.82.6.878

Handley, I.M., & Runnion, B.M. (2011). Evidence that unconscious thinking influences persuasion based on argument quality. *Social Cognition, 29*(6), 668–682.

Hilvert-Bruce, Z., Neill, J.T., Sjöblom, M., & Hamari, J. (2018). Social motivations of live-streaming viewer engagement on Twitch. *Computers in Human Behavior, 84,* 58–67

Hiniker, A., Patel, S.N., Kohno, T., & Kientz, J.A. (2016). Why would you do that? Predicting the uses and gratifications behind smartphone-usage behaviors. In P. Lukowicz & A. Kruger (Eds.), *UbiComp '16: Proceedings of the 2016 ACM International Joint Conference on Pervasive and Ubiquitous Computing*. Heidelberg, Germany.

Hinds, J., & Joinson, A. (2019). Human and computer personality prediction from digital footprints. *Current Directions in Psychological Science, 28*(2), 204–2011. https://doi.org/10.1177/0963721419827849

Ivens, B.S., Leischnig, A., Muller, B., & Valta, K. (2015). On the role of brand stereotypes in shaping consumer response toward brands: An empirical examination of direct and mediating effects of warmth and competence. *Psychology & Marketing, 32*(8), 808–820. https://doi.org/10.1002/mar.20820

Kalyanaraman, S., & Sundar, S.S. (2006). The psychological appeal of personalized online content in Web portals: Does customization affect attitudes and behavior? *Journal of Communication, 56,* 110–132.

Kaye, L.K., Egan, I.M., Rowe, B., & Taylor, J. (2024). A qualitative study exploring behaviours which underpin different types of social media use. *Psychology of Popular Media, 14*(2), 264–275. https://doi.org/10.1037/ppm0000533

Kaye, L.K., Rousaki, A., Joyner, L.C., Barrett, L.A.F., & Orchard, L.J. (2022). The Online Behaviour Taxonomy: A conceptual framework to understand behaviour in computer-mediated communication. *Computers in Human Behavior,* 107443. https://doi.org/10.1016/j.chb.2022.107443

Kervyn, N., Fiske, S.T., & Malone, C. (2022). Social perception of brands: Warmth and competence define images of both brands and social groups. *Consumer Psychology Review, 5*(1), 51–68. https://doi.org/10.1002/arcp.1074

Kirshner, S.N. (2024). GPT and CLT: The impact of ChatGPT's level of abstraction on consumer recommendations. *Journal of Retailing and Consumer Services, 76,* 103580. https://doi.org/10.1016/j.jretconser.2023.103580

Kock, N. (2004). The Psychobiological Model: Towards a new theory of computer-mediated communication based on Darwinian Evolution. *Organization Science, 15*(3), 327–348. https://doi.org/10.1287/orsc.1040.0071

Kock, N. (2005). Media richness or media naturalness? The evolution of our biological communication apparatus and its influence on our behavior toward e-communication tools. *IEEE Transactions on Professional Communication, 48*(2), 117–130. https://doi.org/10.1109/TPC.2005.849649

Kock, N. (2011). Media naturalness theory: Human evolution and behaviour towards electronic communication technologies. In S.C. Roberts (Ed.), *Applied Evolutionary Psychology* (pp. 380–398). Oxford University Press. https://doi.org/10.1093/acprof:oso/9780199586073.003.0023

Kosinski, M., Bachrach, Y., Kohli, P., Stillwell, D., & Graepel, T. (2014). Manifestations of user personality in website choice and behaviour on online social networks. *Machine Learning, 95*(2), 357

LaRose, R., & Eastin, M.S. (2004). A social cognitive theory of internet uses and gratifications: Toward a new model of media attendance. *Journal of Broadcasting and Electronic Media, 48*(3), 358–377.

LaRose, R., Mastro, D., & Eastin, M.S. (2001). Understanding Internet usage: A social-cognitive approach to uses and gratifications. *Social Science Computer Review, 19*(4), 395–413. doi:10.1177/089443930101900401

Lee, M.T. & Theokary, C. (2021). The superstar social media influencer: Exploiting linguistic style and emotional contagion over content? *Journal of Business Research, 132,* 860–871. https://doi.org/10.1016/j.jbusres.2020.11.014

Leong, L-Y., Hew, T-S., Ooi, K-B., & Lin, B. (2019). Do electronic word-of-mouth and elaboration likelihood model influence hotel booking? *Journal of Computer Information Systems, 59*(2), 146–160. https://doi.org/10.1080/08874417.2017.1320953

Li, C-Y. (2013). Persuasive messages on information system acceptance: A theoretical extension of elaboration likelihood model and social influence theory. *Computers in Human Behavior, 29*(1), 164–275. https://doi.org/10.1016/j.chb.2012.09.003

Li, L. & Kang K. (2022). Understanding the real-time interaction between middle-aged consumers and online experts based on the COM-B model. *Journal of Marketing Analytics, 23,* 1–13. https://doi.org/10.1057/s41270-022-00196-1

Liao, L., & Huang, T. (2021). The effect of different social media marketing channels and events on movie box office: An elaboration likelihood model perspective. *Information & Management, 58*(7), e103481. https://doi.org/10.1016/j.im.2021.103481

Marangunić, N., & Granić, A. (2015). Technology acceptance model: A literature review from 1986 to 2013. *Universal Access in the Information Society, 14*(1), 81–95. doi: 10.1007/s10209-014-0348-1

Masuda, H., Han, S.H., & Lee, J. (2022). Impacts of influencer attributes on purchase intentions in social media influencer marketing: Mediating roles of characterizations. *Technological Forecasting and Social Change, 174,* 121246. https://doi.org/10.1016/j.techfore.2021.121246

Meng, K.S., & Leung, L. (2021). Factors influencing TikTok engagement behaviors in China: An examination of gratifications sought, narcissism, and the Big Five personality traits. *Telecommunications Policy, 45*(7), 102172. https://doi.org/10.1016/j.telpol.2021.102172

Michie, S., van Stralen, M.M. & West, R. (2011). The behaviour change wheel: A new method for characterising and designing behaviour change interventions. *Implementation Science, 6,* 42. https://doi.org/10.1186/1748-5908-6-42

Parrott, G., Danbury, A., & Kanthavanich, P. (2015). Online behaviour of luxury fashion brand advocates. *Journal of Fashion Marketing and Management, 19*(4), 360–383. https://doi.org/10.1108/JFMM-09-2014-0069

Pennington, C.R., Murray, E.A.H., Kaye, L.K, Burgess, A., Kessler, K., & Shaw, D.J. (2025). Social competencies mediate relationships between styles of social media usage and psychosocial wellbeing. *Computers in Human Behavior Reports, 19,* 100753. https://doi.org/10.1016/j.chbr.2025.100753

Petty, R., & Cacioppo, J. (1986). The elaboration likelihood model of persuasion. *Advances in Experimental Social Psychology, 19,* 123–205.

Rafaeli, S. (1988). Interactivity: From new media to communication. *Sage Annual Review of Communication Research: Advancing Communication Science,* 16, 110–134.

Sarstedt, M., Adler, S.J., Rau, L., & Schmitt, B. (2024). Using large language models to generate silicon samples in consumer and marketing research: Challenges, opportunities, and guidelines. *Psychology & Marketing, 41*(6), 1254–1270. https://doi.org/10.1002/mar.21982

Shaw, H., Ellis, D.A., & Ziegler, F.V. (2018). The Technology Integration Model (TIM): Predicting the continued use of technology. *Computers in Human Behavior, 83,* 204–214. https://doi.org/10.1016/j.chb.2018.02.001

Shaw, H. (2020). *Examining Individual Differences through 'Everyday' Smartphone Behaviours: Exploring Theories and Methods.* PhD thesis (University of Lincoln).

Shaw, D.J., Kaye, L.K., Ngombe, N., Kessler, K., & Pennington, C.R. (2022). It's not what you do, it's the way that you do it: An experimental task delineates among passive, reactive and interactive styles of behaviour on social networking sites. *PLoS One, 17*(12), e0276765. https://doi.org/10.1371/journal.pone.0276765

Short, J., Williams, E., & Christie, B. (1976). *The Social Psychology of Telecommunications.* London: John Wiley & Sons.

Sundar, S. S. (1998). Effect of source attribution on perception of online news stories. *Journalism & Mass Communication Quarterly, 75*(1), 55–68.

Sundar, S.S. (2007). Social psychology of interactivity in human-website interaction. In A. Joinson, K. McKenna, T. Postmes, & U. Reips (Eds), *The*

Oxford Handbook of Internet Psychology (pp. 89–102). Oxford: Oxford University Press.

Sundar, S.S. (2000). Multimedia effects on processing and perception of online news: A study of picture, audio, and video downloads. *Journalism & Mass Communication Quarterly*, *77*(3), 480–499.

Sundar, S. S., Kalyanaraman, S., & Brown, J. (2003). Explicating website interactivity: Impression-formation effects in political campaign sites. *Communication Research*, *30*(1), 30–59.

Taylor, S.J., Muchnik, L., Kumar, M., & Aral, S. (2022). Identity effects in social media. *Nature Human Behaviour*, *7*, 27–37. https://doi.org/10.1038/s41562-022-01459-8

Teng, S., Khong, K-W., Goh, W-W., & Chong, A. (2014). Examining the antecedents of persuasive eWOM messages in social media. *Online Information Review*, *38*(6), 746–768. https://doi.org/10.1108/OIR-04-2014-0089

Tucker, C. (2016). Social advertising: How advertising that explicitly promotes social influence can backfire. https://doi.org/10.2139/ssrn.1975897

Venkatesh, V., Thong, J.Y., & Xu, X. (2012). Consumer acceptance and use of information technology: Extending the unified theory of acceptance and use of technology. *MIS Quarterly*, 157–178.

Walther, J.B. (1992). Interpersonal effects in computer-mediated interaction. *Communication Research*, *19*(1), 52–90. https://doi.org/10.1177/009365092019001003

Walther, J.B. (1996). Computer-mediated communication: Impersonal, Interpersonal, and Hyperpersonal Interaction. *Communication Research*, *23*(1), 3–43. https://doi.org/10.1177/009365096023001001

Wang, L., & Lee, J-H. (2019). The effect of K-beauty SNS influencer on Chinese consumers' acceptance intention of new products: Focused on Elaboration Likelihood Model (ELM). *Fashion & Textile Research Journal*, *21*(5), 575–585.

Wang, X., Cheng, M., Zhu, J., & Jiang, R. (2023). When texts meet emoji: A multi-stage study of tourism brands. *Journal of Travel Research* *63*(8), 2062–2077. https://doi.org/10.1177/00472875231203396

Weismueller, J., Harrigan, P., Wang, S., & Soutar, G.N. (2020). Influencer endorsements: How advertising disclosure and source credibility affect consumer purchase intention on social media. *Australasian Marketing Journal*, *28*(4). https://doi.org/10.1016/j.ausmj.2020.03.002

Wind, J., & Rangaswamy, A. (2001). Customerization: The next revolution in mass customization. *Journal of Interactive Marketing*, *15*(1), 13–33.

Woo Yoo, C., Sanders, G.L., & Moon, J. (2013). Exploring the effect of e-WOM participation on e-Loyalty in e-commerce. *Decision Support Systems*, *55*(3), 669–678. https://doi.org/10.1016/j.dss.2013.02.001

Yang, J., & Zhao, X. (2021). The impact of information processing styles and persuasive appeals on consumers' engagement intention toward

social media video ads. *Journal of Promotion Management, 27*(4), 524–546. https://doi.org/10.1080/10496491.2020.1851846
Zawisza, M., & Pittard, C. (2015). When do warmth and competence sell best? The "Golden quadrant" shifts as a function of congruity with the product type, targets' individual differences, and advertising appeal type. *Basic and Applied Social Psychology, 37*(2), 131–141.
Zhao, S., Grasmuck, S., & Martin, J. (2008). Identity construction on Facebook: Digital empowerment in anchored relationships. *Computers in Human Behavior, 24*(5), 1816–1836. https://doi.org/10.1016/j.chb.2008.02.012
Zheng, S., Cui, J., Sun, C., Li, J., Li, B., & Guan W. (2022). The effects of the type of information played in environmentally themed short videos on social media on people's willingness to protect the environment. *International Journal of Environmental Research and Public Health, 19*(15), 9520. https://doi.org/10.3390/ijerph19159520
Zillmann, D. (1988a). Mood management: Using entertainment to full advantage. In L. Donohew, H.E. Sypher, & E.T. Higgins (Eds). *Communication, Social Cognition and Affect* (pp. 147–171). Hillsdale, NJ: Lawrence Erlbaum Associates.
Zillmann, D. (1988b). Mood management through communication choices. *American Behavioral Scientist, 31*, 327–340.
Zillmann, D., & Bryant, J. (1985). Affect, mood, and emotion as determinants of selective exposure. In D. Zillmann, & J. Bryant (Eds) *Selective Exposure to Communication* (pp. 157–190). Hillsdale, NJ: Lawrence Erlbaum Associates.

Chapter 5

Health cyberpsychology

Outline and definition of the theme

Health cyberpsychology is the intersection between cyberpsychology, health psychology, and digital health/well-being. Broadly speaking, this is focused on the human experience of using technology and the Internet in respect of how this relates to both physical and psychological health and well-being. Within an occupational context, this might also intersect with the impact of workplace technology with stress management, employee well-being, and work–life balance. However, these types of issues are discussed in further detail in Chapter 6 on industrial-organisational cyberpsychology.

The domain of Health Psychology provides significant insights into the psychology of health and well-being, but perhaps the introduction of cyberpsychology can offer some advancement. Namely, it can provide a more nuanced understanding of the psychological affordances of the user experience when using technology and the Internet to explain *how* and *why* this might be related to health and well-being, rather than simply *what* the impacts might be. For example, cyberpsychology can draw on the extent to which features and functions of digital health and well-being technology might be efficacious, and how digital behaviours translate into "real world" behaviours (and vice versa) in relation to physical health behaviours. This is especially useful when considering the fact that many physical and psychological health interventions include forms of digital technology, where cyberpsychology might be better placed to understand *why* this is effective rather than just *what* is effective.

DOI: 10.4324/9781003581741-5

Prominent issues

Some of the prominent themes in Health Cyberpsychology relate to digital health and well-being applications (apps), online social support and well-being, social media and well-being, and digital twins. Each of these is detailed below to indicate the practical value these insights can bring to various sectors and careers.

Digital health and well-being apps

Digital health and well-being apps largely refer to any applications on smart devices which are built with the intention of supporting users' physical or psychological health and well-being. These can be referred to by many names including: MHealth apps, MedTech, E-Health, HealthTech or Well-being Tech. Broadly speaking, digital health and well-being apps are positioned to support health and well-being in a number of ways, depending on the specific features and functions of the app. Some functions include:

- Self-monitoring tools to measure behaviour related to physical health outcomes such as diet diaries, smartwatches, fitness apps (e.g., Strava)
- Self-monitoring tools to measure behaviour related to psychological well-being outcomes (e.g., MoodPath)
- Delivering therapeutic services or treatment via online means, such as mindfulness, relaxation, breathing exercises (e.g., HeadSpace, Calm)
- Providing information and resources relating to health and well-being (e.g., StayAlive)
- Providing social support and community functions relating to health and well-being (often consisting of community features built into well-being apps)

There has been considerable research which has explored the effectiveness of digital health and well-being apps (Bakker et al., 2016; Simon & Ludman, 2009). Much of this has evidenced that consumers generally have positive perspectives about the use of such apps (Gaffney et al., 2019; Rathbone et al., 2017; Szinay et al., 2021). In respect of their efficacy for mental health-related outcomes, however, the research presents mixed findings. While some research demonstrates that they can reduce depressive and anxiety symptoms and increase mental well-being (Bakker & Rickard, 2018), other studies question their capacity to effectively support individuals with specific well-being and mental health concerns (Grist et al., 2017). Additionally, there are few comprehensive reviews examining the efficacy of apps designed to facilitate improvements in mental health and overall well-being (Eisenstadt et al., 2021; Sucala et al., 2017).

These limitations present key opportunities for cyberpsychology-related contributions to more fully review how and why different types of digital apps and interventions might (or might not) be effective. Particularly, this might offer insights into the enablers of user acceptance which could be integrated into the development process if cyberpsychologists were part of collaborative development teams. While apps offer features aimed at promoting mental well-being, the specific focus, depth and customisability of these features may differ depending on an app's purpose and target audience, leading to differences in usage rates attributable to these factors (Baumel et al., 2019). Having these insights might enhance user engagement, and build further understanding of how users' interactions with different features and functions of different types of apps might explain what specific UX components are especially important in this context. Research suggests that technology adoption is a multifaceted process shaped by social dynamics, individual perceptions, and factors such as coherence, usefulness, and ease of use (Straub, 2009; Yapa et al., 2019). All these factors relate to the decision-making that users negotiate in initial digital acceptance which are fundamental to subsequent engagement, so therefore can be something cyberpsychologists can help recognise and account for in user testing and onboarding processes. Additionally, collaborating with cyberpsychologists might help evaluate how features of smartphone-enabled apps such as context sensing, continuous accessibility, notifications, and so on might relate to UX and behavioural engagement and related health outcomes (Weisel et al., 2019).

On a more basic level, cyberpsychologists might be well placed to offer advice on what conceptual models of digital "engagement" can refer to and how these operate both on a psychological and behavioural level. Yardley et al. (2016) proposed distinguishing between micro- and macro-level engagement in user interactions with interventions. Micro-level engagement might involve users' direct interactions, while macro-level engagement could relate more to a deeper involvement with behaviour change processes and digital intervention goals. Therefore cyberpsychologically informed insights regarding UX can draw out the complexities surrounding digital app efficacy, reliability, and ultimately, better integration of apps into healthcare practice.

Digital games and health

A related area of literature in cyberpsychology is in the field of applied or serious digital games, specifically in relation to health and well-being outcomes. There is a wide literature which has explored the effectiveness of games when used to support a variety of physical and psychological health experiences (Ceranoglu, 2010; Colder Carras et al., 2018; Douris et al., 2012; Wols et al., 2024). "Applied games" (sometimes referred to as "serious games") are games which are designed specifically towards a strategic end goal for patient/user outcomes rather than the use of recreational or commercial games, which are not specifically designed for supporting health-related outcomes. The mechanisms by which games can be effective in a health context may be multifaceted. That is, any type of game which is engaging (whether this is an applied game or one "off-the-shelf") may provide distraction such as from negative health-related symptoms such as pain or intrusive thoughts (Burns-Nader et al., 2017; Dwairej et al., 2018). Additionally, the motivating, interactive, and engaging nature of games in general, make them effective in encouraging things like physical movement as is the case in exergames such as via the WiFit or Xbox Connect. However, serious games, designed specifically to target a particular condition are likely to hold alternative benefits such as acceptance and literacy of one's condition, motivating health-related behaviours, better self-monitoring and regulation of attitudes and behaviours relating to supporting recovery from a condition, and much more.

Similarly to the above on digital apps, cyberpsychological insight can be especially useful to help unpick the various factors and mechanisms which might account for how and why digital games (and their complexities) might relate to different health-related outcomes. Understanding the UX associated with different game features both at device level and game software level can identity what the key components are which relate to motivation and engagement at a level beyond the behavioural level. Alternatively, cyberpsychologists' understanding of the complexities of the academic literature on the psychology of video games means they are well placed to tackle public debates and policy discussions relating to effects of games. In this way, they can provide useful evidence-informed summaries of what current knowledge is relating to this research area, which can serve as useful knowledge for informing policy development and practitioner guidance on appropriate use of digital games in various contexts.

Online social support

Within the academic literature, there is a wealth of research on the topic of online social support. Within this, this broadly seeks to understand different forms of social support which can be garnered via technology or the Internet. This can include: informational support, emotional support via online interaction functions, and support via sense of community and shared identity. For example, research has studied the benefits of social media for those with dementia and their carers, and its impact on identity formation (Talbot et al., 2021), and for sharing experiences and stories of having dementia (Bartmess et al., 2022; Talbot & Coulson, 2023). Other research has explored the use of online forums for those with intellectual disabilities and their carers, and how this relates to identity experiences (Chadwick & Fullwood, 2018), and experiences of inclusion (Chadwick & Buell, 2023). In relation to physical health, other research has focused on online peer support via online forums to explore how these can be supportive for those with physical or psychological health issues such as: HIV/AIDs (Coulson & Buchanan, 2022), Multiple sclerosis (Gerritzen et al., 2022), Tourette syndrome and tic disorders (Soós et al., 2022), and Huntington's disease (Smedley & Coulson, 2021).

These insights can be especially useful for informing how online forums might be best used as a complement to physical and psychological healthcare information and treatment provision. For example, this might include offering insights about what type of support might be most useful for different types of forum user, or informing forum moderator guidance on how they might be best situated to managing forums for optimal experiences of users. Alternatively, insights about the benefits which can come from online forums is also useful for informing parents or carers, especially those who may be caring for people with challenging issues, on how they can best make use of online forums as a support for themselves in their caring roles. As such, this can inform evidence-based guidance provided by charities or other organisations to help those in caring roles.

Social media and well-being

There is an extensive literature on the topic of social media and well-being (see Ferguson et al., 2024). The majority of the literature focuses on correlating volume of social media use (e.g., average hours per day spent on social media) with mental health variables such as depression, anxiety, loneliness, and suicide ideation. The literature remains highly volatile with mixed findings regarding the links between social media use and well-being. The mixed findings are largely attributed to inconsistent conceptual understanding and measurement across studies of what "social media use" actually refers to (Kaye, 2021; Kaye et al., 2024). This is where cyberpsychological insight can be extremely useful, to help recognise the complexities of behaviours which underpin "social media use", and why measuring these is important for understanding how differences in social media use account for differential impacts on user well-being (Pennington et al., 2025; Shaw et al., 2022). Additionally, given the volatile and mixed nature of the academic literature on this issue, cyberpsychologists are well placed to navigate this to provide evidence-informed insights to inform practitioner guidance, public debate, and policy discussions on this topic. Relatedly, in a context in which social technology companies are being held to account for causing harm to users, being able to contribute a cyberpsychologically-informed critical appraisal of the evidence-base to gauge its robustness, rigour, and causality remains highly relevant.

As a practical example, Case Studies 11 and 12 introduce Dr Cath Knibbs and Jennifer Kyalo who are in the domains of Counselling and Clinical Psychology, respectively. Their engagement with the cyberpsychology literature ensures they adopt an evidence-informed approach to therapeutic practice when supporting young people, their parents and practitioners. Additionally, Case Studies 13 and 14 introduce Dr Rachel Wood and Saba Oji who both have a focus on the intersection of AI within therapeutic practice, albeit in different ways.

Case study 11 Dr Catherine Knibbs: Child Trauma Psychotherapist (Cyber Trauma) at Children and Tech

Qualifications

- PhD in Psychotherapy and Counselling (current)
- MSc in Child & Adult Integrative Psychotherapy
- MSc in Psychotherapy Dual Register

How Cath applies cyberpsychology

- Undertaking psychotherapy techniques to support children experiencing trauma-related experiences
- Delivering Cybertrauma ® programmes and courses on online harms
- Writing on the topic of cybertrauma to help inform the general public, parents and therapists about how to protect and support children in online spaces

More information: https://www.cybercology.com/2024/07/31/catherine-knibbs-ep7/

Case study 12 Jennifer Kyalo: Psychologist at Safe Space Arena

Qualifications

- PsyD (current) in Clinical Psychology
- MA in Counseling Psychology
- BA in Counseling Psychology

Networks

- Registered member of the Counselors and Psychologists Board of Kenya
- Graduate Student member of the American Psychological Association

How Jennifer applies cyberpsychology

- Assessment and diagnosis: assessing clients' screen time, online relationship patterns, internet addiction, gaming patterns, social media dependence as a coping tool or distraction, and how they generally engage with the internet, as part of clinical evaluation, especially when dealing with mood disorders
- Treatment delivery: providing online therapy sessions, as well as producing mental health psychoeducation content on the internet
- Therapeutic interventions: using cyberpsychology subject knowledge to help clients develop healthier relationships with technology and social media. (e.g., recommend apps that help clients keep track of their moods, journaling apps, and other self-care resources that are digital)

More information: https://www.linkedin.com/in/jenniferkyalo/

Case study 13 Dr Rachel Wood: Founder of AI Mental Health Collective

Qualifications

- PhD in Cyberpsychology

How Rachel applies cyberpsychology

- Combining clinical background in mental health with research in cyberpsychology (specifically AI) to raise awareness and create cross-discipline dialogue and collaboration at the intersection of AI and mental health

More information: www.dr-rachelwood.com

Case study 14 Saba Oji: Founder/CEO of HolisticMindAI Inc.

Qualifications

- PhD in Public Health (current)
- MSc in Biomedical Sciences
- BSc (Hons) in Health Studies with Gerontology Minor
- Diploma (Data Science)
- Diploma (Web Development)
- Certificate (Cybersecurity & Digital Health Training for Health Science Professionals)

How Saba applies cyberpsychology

- Applying cyberpsychology principles to design AI-powered tools that strengthen the therapeutic relationship between clients and clinicians
- Using generative AI to transcribe and summarise therapy sessions and create personalised AI companions that support reflection, continuity of care, and client engagement between visits
- Integrating trust, digital empathy, and user autonomy into AI-assisted mental health workflows, ensuring human connection and ethical oversight remain central to all

interactions. These applications translate cyberpsychology theories of online behaviour, human–AI trust, and digital well-being into real-world clinical technology

More information: https://holisticmindai.com/

Digital twins

Digital twins are models in the form of digital representations which mirror physical objects or people. Whilst digital twins are being applied across a range of sectors, their role within healthcare is especially prominent. Particularly, they can use population-level patient data to create virtual replicas to help make models, create predictions, and form simulations of how treatment scenarios might play out. With the use of real-time patient data, these can be dynamic based on being able to continuously update and adapt, in a data-driven manner. Within healthcare, these can provide data-driven insights to help model health risk factors based on patient characteristics (e.g., ethnicity), inform treatment decisions, reduce risks to patients, and more generally help improve patient outcomes. Whilst this is not specifically a focus of research in the academic cyberpsychology literature, it provides some clear examples of how the use of (digital) data relating to patients, and AI-based models are being harnessed within healthcare organisations, in the interests of improving patient experiences and outcomes.

Summary of key impacts of cyberpsychology

Here is a summary of the key impacts from these key themes in the research literature and Case Studies:

- **Public health sector** – evidence-based insights can help inform practitioners about how best to apply apps and digital games within therapeutic practice. Specifically understanding the user acceptance and UX related mechanisms which might apply to different types of apps or games, and the impact this might have on engagement beyond the behavioural level

- **Therapeutic applications** – using evidence-based insights within therapeutic practice, including informing healthy relationships with technology and supporting impacts associated with online harm and cyber-trauma
- **Technology sector** – evidence-based insights on efficiency of apps/products. This can help inform their development and user testing processes to better understand engagement and UX
- **Community managers and moderators** – supporting evidence-informed guidance for practitioners, moderators, community groups and charities on how to optimise engagement with online forums as a complementary support mechanism
- **Legal sector** – helping navigate and establish the validity of the evidence-base making claims about social media harms

Advice

As outlined in Chapter 3, ensuring you are translating your insights into language that makes sense to your target clients or groups is key to being successful when engaging people as an independent consultant. In the case of health cyberpsychology, the types of clients are likely to include public health organisations, charities, digital health and well-being technology companies, or patients/clients (in the case of those who are clinically or therapeutically qualified). Some indicative examples of types of insights that relate to these include:

- Public sector (e.g., public health, health councils, health education services) – delivering and evaluating digital health services or provision, implementing digital health education programmes, informing public health policy regarding digital health and well-being
- Charity and third sector (e.g., well-being charities, children's advocacy groups, online safety advocacy groups, etc) – providing evaluation or research on digital issues in society, delivering educational campaigns to raise public awareness relating to digital health or well-being, using research evidence to inform policy and practice
- Technology sector (e.g., Digital Health and Well-being Tech companies) – conducting research or user testing on digital

health products or services, evaluating the effectiveness of digital health technologies on patient or user outcomes
- Therapeutic settings – engaging in scholarship to use evidence-informed approaches to client services

Here are key areas which are worth doing some self-study on, to better understand the types of things that organisations will be interested in. Some of these might include:

- Evaluation – measuring whether any health/well-being education or campaigns have been successful to demonstrate the value of the organisation
- Campaigns – focused messages surrounding a theme or agenda to encourage public engagement with an initiative or service
- Policy development – developing documentation and a set of principles, recommendations and/or actions relating to a thematic area (e.g., online safety). Best practice on this is that the actions/recommendations are evidence-informed from primary research or evaluation
- Stakeholder engagement – methods of engaging with people who might be beneficiaries of the work of the organisation or be partners to support the operations of the organisation
- Trustee or annual reports – for charities, compiling trustee reports is an annual process, to document evidence about the impact of the charity's activities. Best practice here might relate to using different types of data to evidence this impact.

Indicative keywords and job roles

- User Researcher
- Innovation Scientist
- Intervention Scientist
- Project Manager
- Patient Engagement Officer
- Patient Evaluation Officer
- Service User Engagement Officer
- Evaluation Officer/Coordinator
- Project Officer/Coordinator
- (Digital) Wellness Officer

- Well-being Practitioner
- MedTech
- E-Health
- MHealth
- HealthTech
- Well-being Tech

Resources

Centre for Health Technology (2025). *Digital Health Resources for Clinicians and Researchers*. https://arc-swp.nihr.ac.uk/research/projects/digital-health-resources/

Digital Wellbeing blog. https://digitalwellbeing.org/author/marsattacks/

Knibbs, C. (2023). *Online Harms and Cybertrauma: Legal and Harmful Issues with Children and Young People*. Routledge

UK Parliament (2025). *Digital twins – dynamic models that respond to real-time data*. Retrieved September 22, 2025, from https://post.parliament.uk/digital-twins-dynamic-models-that-respond-to-real-time-data/

WHO (2025). *Global Initiative on Digital Health* – https://www.who.int/initiatives/gidh

References

Bakker, D., Kazantzis, N., Rickwood, D., & Rickard, N. (2016). Mental health smartphone apps: Review and evidence-based recommendations for future developments. *JMIR Mental Health, 3*(1), e4984.

Bakker, D., & Rickard, N. (2018). Engagement in mobile phone app for self-monitoring of emotional wellbeing predicts changes in mental health: MoodPrism. *Journal of Affective Disorders, 227*, 432–442. https://doi.org/10.1016/j.jad.2017.11.016.

Bartmess, M., Talbot, C., O'Dwyer, S.T., Lopez, R.P., Rose, K.M. & Anderson, J.G. (2022). Using Twitter to understand perspectives and experiences of dementia and caregiving at the beginning of the COVID-19 pandemic. *Dementia, 21*(5), 1734–1752.

Baumel, A., Muench, F., Edan, S., & Kane, J.M. (2019). Objective user engagement with mental health apps: Systematic search and panel-based usage analysis. *Journal of Medical Internet Research, 21*(9), e14567.

Burns-Nader, S., Joe, L., & Pinion, K. (2017). Computer tablet distraction reduces pain and anxiety in pediatric burn patients undergoing hydrotherapy: A randomized trial. *Burns, 43*, 1203–1211.

Ceranoglu, T.A. (2010). Video games in psychotherapy. *Review of General Psychology*, 14, 141–146.

Chadwick, D.D. & Buell, S. (2023) Interactional power and support in digital inclusion of an adult with intellectual disabilities: A case study analysis. *Journal of Research in Special Educational Needs, 23*, 251–261. https://doi.org/10.1111/1471-3802.12596

Chadwick, D., & Fullwood, C. (2018). An online life like any other: Identity, self-determination, and social networking among adults with intellectual disabilities. *Cyberpsychology, Social Networking and Behavior, 21*(1), 56–64.

Colder Carras, M., Van Rooij, A.J., Spruijt-Metz, D., Kvedar, J., Griffiths, M.D., Carabas, Y., & Labrique, A. (2018). Commercial video games as therapy: A new research agenda to unlock the potential of a global pastime. *Frontiers in Psychiatry, 8*, 300. https://doi.org/10.3389/fpsyt.2017.00300

Coulson, N.S., & Buchanan, H. (2022). The role of online support groups in supporting individuals affected by HIV/AIDS: A scoping review of the literature. *Journal of Medical Internet Research, 24*(7), e27648

Douris, P.C., McDonald, B., Vespi, F., Kelley, N.C., & Herman, L. (2012). Comparison between Nintendo Wii Fit aerobics and traditional aerobic exercise in sedentary young adults. *The Journal of Strength & Conditioning Research, 26*(4), 1052–1057. https://doi.org/10.1519/JSC.0b013e31822e5967

Dwairej, D., Obeidat, H., & Khalaf, I. (2018). The effectiveness of video distraction on children preoperative anxiety: An integrative literature review. *Open Journal of Nursing, 8*(3), 171–187. https://doi.org/10.4236/ojn.2018.83015

Eisenstadt, M., Liverpool, S., Infanti, E., Ciuvat, R.M., & Carlsson, C. (2021). Mobile apps that promote emotion regulation, positive mental health, and well-being in the general population: Systematic review and meta-analysis. *JMIR Mental Health, 8*(11), e31170.

Ferguson, C.J., Kaye, L.K., Branley-Bell, D., & Markey, P. (2024). There is no evidence that social media use is correlated with adolescent mental health problems: Findings from a meta-analysis. *Professional Psychology: Research and Practice 56*(1), 73–83. https://doi.org/10.1037/pro0000589

Gaffney, H., Mansell, W., & Tai, S. (2019). Conversational agents in the treatment of mental health problems: Mixed-method systematic review. *JMIR Mental Health, 6*(10), e14166.

Gerritzen, E., Lee, A., McDermoot, O., Coulson, N.S., & Orrell, M. (2022). Online peer support for people with Multiple Sclerosis: A narrative synthesis systematic review. *International Journal of MS Care, 24*(6), 252–259.

Grist, R., Porter, J., & Stallard, P. (2017). Mental health mobile apps for preadolescents and adolescents: Asystematic review. *Journal of Medical Internet Research, 19*(5), e176.

Kaye, L.K. (2021). Exploring "socialness" in social media. *Computers in Human Behavior Reports, 3*. 100083. https://doi.org/10.1016/j.chbr.2021.100083

Kaye, L.K., Egan, I.M., Rowe, B., & Taylor, J. (2024). A qualitative study exploring behaviours which underpin different types of social media use. *Psychology of Popular Media, 14*(2), 264–275. https://doi.org/10.1037/ppm0000533

Pennington, C.R., Murray, E.A.H., Kaye, L.K, Burgess, A., Kessler, K., & Shaw, D.J. (2025). Social competencies mediate relationships between styles of social media usage and psychosocial wellbeing. *Computers in Human Behavior Reports, 19*, 100753. https://doi.org/10.1016/j.chbr.2025.100753

Rathbone, A.L., Clarry, L., & Prescott, J. (2017). Assessing the efficacy of mobile health apps using the basic principles of cognitive behavioral therapy: systematic review. *Journal of Medical Internet Research, 19*(11), e399.

Shaw, D.J., Kaye, L.K., Ngombe, N., Kessler, K., & Pennington, C.R. (2022). It's not what you do, it's the way that you do it: An experimental task delineates among passive, reactive and interactive styles of behaviour on social networking sites. *PLoS One, 17*(12), e0276765. https://doi.org/10.1371/journal.pone.0276765

Simon, G.E., & Ludman, E.J. (2009). It's time for disruptive innovation in psychotherapy. *The Lancet, 374*(9690), 594–595.

Smedley, R.M. & Coulson, N.S., (2021). Genetic testing for Huntington's disease: A thematic analysis of online support community messages. *Journal of Health Psychology, 26*(4), 580–594.

Soós, M.J., Coulson, N.S., & Davies, E.B. (2022). Exploring social support in an online support community for Tourette Syndrome and Tic disorders: Analysis of postings. *Journal of Medical Internet Research, 24*(10), e34403. https://doi.org/10.2196/34403

Straub, E. (2009). Understanding technology adoption: Theory and future directions for informal learning. *Review of Educational Research, 79*, 625–649. https://doi.org/10.3102/0034654308325896.

Sucala, M., Cuijpers, P., Muench, F., Cardoş, R., Soflau, R., Dobrean, A., … & David, D. (2017). Anxiety: There is an app for that. A systematic review of anxiety apps. *Depression and Anxiety, 34*(6), 518–525.

Szinay, D., Perski, O., Jones, A., Chadborn, T., Brown, J., & Naughton, F. (2021). Perceptions of factors influencing engagement with health and well-being apps in the United Kingdom: Qualitative interview study. *JMIR mHealth and uHealth, 9*(12), e29098.

Talbot, C.V., & Coulson, N.S. (2023). "I found it the only place that spoke the same language": A thematic analysis of messages posted to an online peer support forum for people living with dementia. *Age & Ageing, 52*, 1–8.

Talbot, C.V., O'Dwyer, S.T., Clare, L., & Heaton, J. (2021). The use of Twitter by people with young-onset dementia: A qualitative analysis of narratives and identity formation in the age of social media. *Dementia, 20*(7), 2542–2557. https://doi.org/10.1177/14713012211002410.

Weisel, K.K., Fuhrmann, L.M., Berking, M., Baumeister, H., Cuijpers, P., & Ebert, D.D. (2019). Standalone smartphone apps for mental health—a systematic review and meta-analysis. *NPJ Digital Medicine, 2*(1), 118.

Wols, A., Pingel, M., Lichtwarck-Ashoff., & Granic, I. (2024). Effectiveness of applied and casual games for young people's mental health: A systematic review of randomised controlled studies. *Clinical Psychology Review, 108*, 102396. https://doi.org/10.1016/j.cpr.2024.102396

Yapa, S., Senathiraja, R., Poesche, J., & Kauranen, I. (2019). Why adoption of some technologies is faster? An explanation through sequential coherence. *Sri Lanka Journal of Management Studies*. https://doi.org/10.4038/sljms.v1i2.49.

Yardley, L., Spring, B.J., Riper, H., Morrison, L.G., Crane, D.H., Curtis, K., ... & Blandford, A. (2016). Understanding and promoting effective engagement with digital behavior change interventions. *American Journal of Preventive Medicine, 51*(5), 833–842.

Chapter 6

Industrial-organisational cyberpsychology

Outline and definition of the theme

Industrial-organisational (I-O) Psychology is a field that applies psychological principles to understand and improve human behaviour, experiences, and performance in the workplace. I-O Psychology might also be referred to as Occupational Psychology or Organisational Psychology, the latter terms perhaps being more typically used in the UK context. I-O psychologists apply their insights by helping organisations with issues such as: workforce planning, talent management, training, leadership development, employee motivation, team dynamics, and change management. More specifically in respect of I-O *cyber*psychology, in the context of workplaces and work practices becoming increasingly digitalised, there is a need to understand how this might intersect with the range of organisational activities and what impacts this may have on the individual employee or employer level, but also on a wider organisational, sector or even Governmental level. There are many ways that organisations transform to become more digitalised. Some of the aspects of I-O Psychology which cyberpsychology is particularly well suited to supporting include: employee selection, distributed working, digital well-being and finally, digital transformation and innovation.

Some of the ways which I-O Psychology is said to improve organisations is by increasing productivity (via implementing more efficient processes, up-skilling employees, etc.), reducing employee turnover (e.g., by understanding the reasons for dissatisfaction), and increasing employee well-being (e.g., by understanding what might a positive environment). The next sections outline where cyberpsychology

DOI: 10.4324/9781003581741-6

might be most relevant to key aspects of I-O Psychology practice, in the context of how increased digitisation might transform employee experiences, workplace practices. and organisational systems.

Employee selection

In relation to employee selection, I-O Psychologists might typically help develop and implement effective hiring and selection processes to ensure that the right individuals match the right roles. There is significant merit in the use of digital methods within recruitment and selection. In the context of the majority of job recruitment being via digital means (e.g., recruitment websites, LinkedIn), this opens up various intriguing possibilities, particularly in making use of Artificial Intelligence (AI) within these processes. AI might be involved for example in advertising vacancies, screening applicants, undertaking assessments, and candidate matching. More specifically, this might entail the use of AI-assisted recruitment software which can automate hiring workflows (e.g., Workable). Another level might be to include AI-driven role profiling which can efficiently identify the important elements of a role being advertised (e.g., Saville Assessment). Alternatively, there may be elements of AI-assisted matching which matches candidates to job vacancies. Indeed, there are already companies such as The MatchBox and Recruitly which do just this. Criteria for match-fit for example, might be based on things like skills, experience, cultural fit, and personal preferences. However, more sophisticated AI-systems might make use of open-AI for semantic searches so a match can still be established with semantically related words or concepts, rather than by exact keyword match. Not only can these systems increase efficiencies in the selection process, they can also identify more relevant applicants and in other cases, increase successful matching relative to traditional selection methods (Budhwar et al., 2022; Faugoo, 2024; Ore & Sposato, 2021; Rab-Kettler & Lehnervp, 2019). However, as is often the case with AI-related discussions, the academic literature on these innovations has drawn attention to the potential risks and ethical implications of AI-assisted or enabled selection processes, particularly in relation to issues such as potential bias (Hunkenschroer & Luetge, 2022; Tippins et al., 2021; Yam & Skorburg, 2021).

Whilst there appears to be an emerging use of AI-assisted systems within recruitment and selection, there is the potential that these could be taken further, perhaps also to integrate elements of psychometrics into the process. Theoretically, open-AI could scrape applicant data from a range of online sources such as from their social media profiles or Google profiles, to generate a psychometric profile to inform any matching processes. The use of "cyberpsychometrics" in this regard could go a step further than submitted documentation to a recruitment site, and instead draw upon any unrestricted online data which might be available about an applicant. I mused about this in a hypothetical piece for the British Psychological Society in 2020, about what psychology might look like in 2040. In the piece, "When the job hunts you", I outlined "auto-generated psychometric profiling" (AGPP), a method whereby users sign up to an AGPP-compliant recruitment agency. The agency has access to their psychometric profile which is updated in real-time, garnered from their online data. When new jobs are advertised anywhere online, the agency automatically corroborates this information, and the potential candidate is notified of a "match-fit" to a given opportunity. Whilst I do not believe such methods are currently being used, there are intriguing potential innovations here to consider.

A final intriguing notion is the use of AI-enabled biometrics within recruitment. Whilst biometrics are traditionally used as part of identification, authentication, and verification, additional behavioural biometrics via smartphones can provide additional contextual information regarding individuals. Specifically, behavioural biometrics such as how much pressure the individual applies to their device, how they hold their device, and scrolling behaviour might all be indicative about an individual's capabilities regarding aspects of job performance (Hinckley et al., 2000). In this context, it is pertinent to ensure there is a solid evidence base to underpin the validity of using these behaviours as part of selection processes. Specifically, having rigorous evidence that these digital behaviours are accurate in determining user characteristics and performance.

This is where cyberpsychology has much to offer. In respect of understanding user characteristics based on digital and online behaviour, research within cyberpsychology has explored how we can garner psychographic characteristics of users from digital behaviour. Indeed, the field of digital traces within this domain has spear-headed efforts in this regard (Rafaeli et al., 2019). For example, digital behaviours from smartphones have been found to predict various personality characteristics (Hinds & Joinson, 2019; Settanni et al., 2018) as well as be informative about people's movement behaviour and life outcomes (Digutsch et al., 2025; Hinds et al., 2021). For example, smartphone behaviours can predict personality traits such as authoritarianism, as well as occupational traits such as procrastination, task performance, and job satisfaction (Digutsch et al., 2025). In respect of life outcomes, recent research has found that models of smartphone behaviour surpass personality trait self-assessments for predicting outcomes such as level of education, and substance abuse (Digutsch et al., 2025). As such, within organisational selection and recruitment processes, cyberpsychology is going to continue to form an important evidence base for determining the validity of alternative forms of psychometrics profiling or screening such as via digital behaviour.

Case Study 15 introduces Dr Genevieve Bartuski who uses their psychological insights to support businesses and clients incorporate new technologies, and consider the ways of ensuring compliance and safety of these.

Case study 15 Dr Genevieve Bartuski: Clinical Forensic Psychologist/Founder/ Privacy and AI Governance Consultant

Qualifications

- PsyD in Clinical Forensic Psychology
- MBA in Business Administration
- MA in Clinical Forensic Psychology
- MSc in Criminal and Penal Psychology
- BA in Forensic Psychology

Networks

- Chartered Psychologist with the British Psychological Society (BPS)

How Genevieve applies cyberpsychology

- Using behavioural science within business consultancy with start-ups and help them build trust and safety right into their designs, with a focus on protecting privacy and reducing psychological harms
- Helping companies develop internal AI policies that take human behaviour into consideration
- Helping organisations adapt new technologies through change management principles
- Within clinical practice, working with parents to help them talk to children about staying safe online
- Consulting with other Clinical Psychologists about AI technologies in practice
- Working with internet safety agencies to develop labels and measurements of harms

More information: https://www.kreinspsyc.com/dr-genevieve-bartuski.html

Distributed working

I-O psychologists might often support organisations with regards to workplace culture and climate to ensure it is positive and productive. In the context of increased digitalisation and its impact on workplace practices, there is increasing demand and appetite for more flexible working arrangements such as remote working which might result in some organisations having a workforce physically situated in rather distributed ways. These workplaces therefore are enabled by a strong reliance on a digital infrastructure which can support agile and flexible working.

However, it might be said that distributed and remote working can bring different challenges with regards to things like team cohesion, communication, collaboration, information security, and productivity. For example, it is known that team cohesion plays a significant role in predicting team performance (Grossman et al., 2021). In distributed relative to co-located working, however, it can be questioned whether team cohesion and communication can be achieved to the same extent

(Hambley et al., 2007). This is where cyberpsychological evidence can be helpful, to draw out the nuances of the social dimensions of human experiences with technology. For example, associated fields such as computer-mediated communication (CMC) advance principles from Social Information Processing Theory whereby it is suggested we use behavioural cues from others as a means of developing relationships and understanding others (Walther, 1992; Walther & D'Addario, 2001). For example, Walther's (1996) hyperpersonal model of communication outlines that online-based communication in some cases may surpass face-to-face equivalents as we might have a tendency to overcompensate for the typical absence of non-verbal cues. Contrary to what we might expect, less rich or natural media may actually permit greater attention to carefully crafted exchanges which might facilitate more careful or effective communication and relationship maintenance.

Other relevant cyberpsychological theories include Media Richness Theory (Daft & Lengel, 1986; Daft et al., 1987) and Media Naturalness Theory (Kock, 2005, 2011). The principles from these theories provide insights into the characteristics of digital media or communications and the impact of user perceptions and experiences. Specifically, Media Richness Theory suggests that communication which increases our perceptual bandwidth such as via multimodal communication (e.g., concurrent visual and audio modalities) would be higher in richness than communications which might be unimodal or text-based (Wang et al., 2023). Four key factors which determine media richness are: i) number of cues being used to convey a message; ii) number of meanings which can be expressed through symbols used; iii) how quickly responses can be issued; and iv) level of personalisation within the message (Daft et al., 1987).

Similarly, Media Naturalness Theory (Kock, 2005, 2011) broadly builds on the aforementioned principles. However, a key distinction is that this refers to the extent to which the behaviour encompassed within a message aligns to what is considered to meet natural communication characteristics. Behaviour which mirrors face-to-face communication is said to be the "gold standard" of natural communication relative to other derivates of communication, such as text-based exchanges. This focuses on five elements of i) high levels of co-location, ii) synchronicity, iii) ability to express and observe facial expressions, iv) express and observe body language and, v) express and listen to speech.

In the case of Media Richness and Media Naturalness, the implication is that communication which has a richer range of behaviours and context would be superior to that which is more unimodal. In the context of distributed working therefore, this might offer evidence to suggest team communication and cohesion might be compromised in this regard. However, it is important to acknowledge that digital communication can represent a wide range of formats (e.g., video conferencing, email, Teams chat etc.), and so it is not necessarily the case that communication would always be simplistic and unimodal. However, a cyberpsychology-based I-O psychologist might be well placed to offer an evidence-based perspective on how and why certain types of digital communication methods might be best situated into different types of work activities, and what impact this might have on things like employee perceptions, engagement, team relationships to name a few.

It is also worth noting that there are wider organisational factors which significantly impact on the extent to which distributed workplaces operate effectively. These can include, leadership, trust, and team identification (Maurer et al., 2022; van der Voet & Steijn, 2020; Wildman et al., 2012). As such, whilst the quality of digital infrastructure and its relationship to team communication and cohesion is important in distributed workplaces, this should not in itself be the only necessary and sufficient factor for efficient and effective distributed working.

Digital well-being

A key part of an I-O psychologist's role might be to design and implement employee well-being initiatives or assess employee satisfaction and well-being. There are various angles in which organisational digitalisation might relate to digital well-being. The first is "technostress", and the second is development of fit-for-purpose digital well-being policies and practices.

In relation to "techno-stress", this broadly relates to the well-being impacts which are associated with technology use. Indeed, it is likely that digital workspaces affect motivation, burnout, and things like surveillance anxiety. Evidence suggests there to be various technostress factors on employee well-being. These include techno-insecurity, techno-overload, techno-uncertainty, techno-complexity, and techno-invasion (Ward et al., 2025). In the workplace, techno-invasion for example, might be attributed to perceptions of constant availability/connectivity, normative response pressure (e.g., with email) and a lack of segregation between work and non-work (Marsh et al., 2022). Of course, these issues might be exacerbated further in distributed workplaces, especially where there might be time-zone disparities across the workforce resulting in blurred boundaries and expectations regarding the time parameters of work practices. As well as impacts on well-being, technostress has been noted to also adversely affect work performance (Würtenberger et al., 2025), indicating this as an organisational-level issue which has implications for digital well-being policies and practices. Clearly, there is an avenue for cyberpsychology to contribute insights to explain the intersection of technology with stress and well-being here. An interesting implication is that whilst organisations might decide to adopt digital tools or systems that optimise productivity, this needs to be considered in the context of how these might impact mental load of employees, which might have a knock-on detrimental impact on their performance and retention. As such, paradoxically, tools designed for productivity might actually reduce productivity as a result.

Interestingly, the majority of psychologically related theories which have been applied to understanding technostress are more general models of stress and coping. These include: the Transactional Model of Stress and Coping (Lazarus and Folkman, 1984), Person–Environment Fit (e.g., Harrison, 1978), and Stressor–Strain–Outcome Model (Koeske & Koeske, 1993). Although these may indeed incorporate relevant principles which can help underpin or explain techno stressors, there may be wider cyberpsychological evidence which can supplement these insights. For example, there may be specific stressors associated with social media use for example, which have unique characteristics which are not fully explained by more traditional theories. As such, the role of a cyberpsychology-informed I-O psychologist might be to draw upon the evidence from cyberpsychology to pin-point what might be specific stressors associated with different types of digital products or services, as a basis for assessing or advising on where specific risks might be in this regard.

In relation to the second strand concerning digital well-being, cyberpsychology may be well placed to inform company digital well-being policies, specifically in relation to ensuring these are evidence-based. Essentially, workplace digital well-being policies are designed to ensure that employees use technology effectively without compromising their health and happiness. This can include some of the aforementioned issues such as promoting work–life balance by encouraging employees to disconnect from work outside of business hours and setting boundaries around technology use. Insights here might be well informed by work on digital disconnection (Vanden Abelle et al., 2024) which offers a much more constructive approach than an all-encompassing "digital detox" which is rarely viable or sustainable. Digital disconnection for example, notes the various challenges associated with digital connection such as boundary-blurring, exposure, time displacement, and inference (Vanden Abelle et al., 2024). Based on these, there can be differentiated disconnection strategies which are sensitive to the contextual determinants of digital connection (e.g., normative expectations to reply). Therefore this can offer a more tailored disconnection approach which is likely to be more effective and sustainable as part of organisational workplace practices.

As a practical example, Case Study 16 introduces Carolyn Freeman who uses cyberpsychological evidence to consult with businesses on healthier digital lifestyles and work practices.

Case study 16 Carolyn Freeman: Workplace Cyberpsychology Practitioner at Cybercology

Qualifications

- MSc in Cyberpsychology
- BSc (Hons) in Psychology
- NDip (Marketing)
- Certificate in Counselling

How Carolyn applies cyberpsychology

- Providing cyberpsychology insights and best practices on how digital technology use affects adults at work, home, and play
- Consulting with businesses to develop solutions to healthier and more balanced digital lifestyles
- Applying therapeutic tools and techniques to support clients to reduce problematic digital technology behaviour
- Writing and pod-casting to raise awareness of cyberpsychology to workplace and corporate contexts

More information: https://www.bps.org.uk/blog/careers-cyberpsychology-conversation-carolyn-freeman

Digital transformation and innovation

The final area where cyberpsychology might be especially helpful towards I-O Psychology practice relates to digital strategy, transformation, and innovation. Indeed, over the last few decades there has been a wealth of research on the topic of technology acceptance which has been widely applied in business and corporate sectors. Broadly, these apply theories which outline the range of socio-cognitive factors associated with users' technology use. These theories include the Technology Acceptance Model (Davis et al., 1989; Marangunić & Granić, 2015), the Unified Theory of Acceptance and Use (Venkatesh et al., 2012), and most recently the Technology Integration Model (Shaw et al., 2018). Broadly, these relate to perceptions about ease of use and usefulness of the technology alongside contextual factors such as facilitating conditions in which the technology may be used.

Whilst these models have tended to focus on issues such as single technology use as a way to understand individual-level adoption, there is merit to how these may be applied on a wider organisational level, especially in the context of digital transformation and innovation. Indeed, the role of a cyberpsychology-informed I-O Psychologist may be well placed to assess employee and organisational attributes in relation to these perceptions about technology acceptance, to support organisational change management in relation to digital transformation or similar. Interestingly, although digital types of transformation and innovation will continue to be a central component of most organisations' change management processes, very few insights from the technology acceptance literature have entered into professional practice. This seems like an obvious segway for cyberpsychology insights to be drawn upon.

Summary of key impacts of cyberpsychology

Here is a summary of the key impacts from these key themes in the research literature and Case Studies:

- **Ensuring effective digital integration and transformation** – cyberpsychology insights can add nuance to more general change management projects or organisational development when there may be new digital systems or processes involved
- **Embedded trust and safety** – cyberpsychology insights can help embed digital safety and enhanced user trust into organisational systems
- **Supporting healthier digital boundaries** – cyberpsychology insights can offer evidence-informed recommendations of how to ensure better work–life boundaries relating to digital workplace technologies

Advice

As outlined in Chapter 3, it is important to translate your insights into language that makes sense to your target clients and groups. In the case of I-O cyberpsychology, the types of clients are likely to include regional or local councils, public sector services (e.g., UK Civil Service), corporate teams, and human resources. Here are key areas which are worth doing some self-study on, to better understand the types of things that organisations will be interested in. Some of these might include:

- Digital transformation – moving aspects of the organisation's operations towards digital systems or solutions
- Change management – a process whereby an organisation has to manage an organisational-level change which often requires a new strategic approach or significant changes in operations

- Skills gap and training – recognising where employee up-skilling or training might be needed, usually to ensure they are able to meet adequate levels of performance or be able to transition into new or adapted roles or organisational requirements
- Recruitment and selection – ensuring that the processes and policies for recruiting new employees is fit for purpose
- Talent acquisition – ensuring that the processes for recruiting new employees is attracting excellent people (i.e. who are highly capable and well-aligned to the organisation and a specific role)
- Regulatory compliance and governance – ensuring the policies and procedures regarding an organisation's legal and non-legal obligations are followed appropriately
- Employee satisfaction and retention – ensuring that employees experience job satisfaction to a level they remain in employment within an organisation
- Productivity – ensuring that work requirements and tasks are undertaken in a way which is efficient and effective towards the strategic objectives of an organisation
- Performance management – ensuring the policies and procedures regarding measuring employee performance are appropriate and implemented effectively

Indicative keywords and job roles

- Digital Workplace Psychologist
- Workforce Analytics Specialist
- Digital Transformation Officer
- Evidence Reviewer
- Evaluation Officer/Coordinator
- Project Officer/Coordinator
- Policy and Evaluation Officer
- Project Manager
- Human factors
- Digital adoption
- Digital strategy
- Technology-enabled business practices
- Technology diffusion
- Digital innovation
- Innovation scientist

Resources

APA (2021). *Careers in Applied Psychology: Industrial-Organizational Psychology:* https://youtu.be/8JfMU6LDoCc

BPS (2020). When the job hunts you: https://www.bps.org.uk/psychologist/when-job-hunts-you

Cybercology. *Digital Work*: https://www.cybercology.com/digital-work/

Schellmann, H. (2024). *The Algorithm: How AI Can Hijack Your Career and Steal Your Future*. C Hurst & Co Publishers Ltd.

Society for Industrial and Organizational Psychology – https://www.siop.org/

SIOP Official (2019). *Five Minute Career Preview: I-O Psychology* – https://www.youtube.com/watch?v=DLR6eCrLih0

References

Budhwar, P., Malik, A., De Silva, M.T.T., & Thevisuthan, P. (2022). Artificial intelligence–challenges and opportunities for international HRM: a review and research agenda. *The International Journal of Human Resource Management, 33*(6), 1065–1097. https://doi.org/10.1080/09585192.2022.2035161

Daft, R.L., & Lengel, R.H. (1986). Organizational Information requirements, media richness and structural design. *Management Science, 32*(5), 554–571. https://doi.org/10.1287/mnsc.32.5.554

Daft, R.L., Lengel, R.H., & Trevino, L.K. (1987). Message equivocality, media selection, and manager performance: Implications for information systems. *MIS Quarterly, 11*(3), 355–366. https://doi.org/10.2307/248682

Davis, F.D., Bagazzie, R.P., & Warshaw, P.R. (1989). User acceptance of computer technology: A comparison of two theoretical model authors. *INFORMS, 35*(8), 982–1003.

Digutsch, J., Sust, L., Schoedel, R., Buehner, M., Koch, T., Bergmann, M., Aluffi, P. A., Racek, D., & Stachl, C. (2025). Everyday Smartphone behaviors predict life outcomes. https://doi.org/10.31234/osf.io/x95em_v2

Faugoo, D. (2024). AI-driven recruitment and selection: Enhanced HR decision-making with accrued benefits of organizational success. *International Journal of Business and Technology Management*, 6(3), 529–536.

Grossman, R., Nolan, K., Rosch, Z., Mazer, D., & Salas, E. (2021). The team cohesion-performance relationship: A meta-analysis exploring measurement approaches and the changing team landscape. *Organizational Psychology Review, 12*(2), 181–238. https://doi.org/10.1177/20413866211041157

Hambley L.A., O'Neill T.A., Kline T.J.B. (2007). Virtual team leadership: The effects of leadership style and communication medium on team interaction styles and outcomes. *Organizational Behavior & Human Decision Processes, 103*(1), 1–20.

Harrison, R.V. (1978). Person-environment fit and job stress. *Stress at Work,* 175–205.

Hinckley, K., Pierce, J., Sinclair, M., & Horvitz, E. (2000). Sensing techniques for mobile interaction. In *Proceedings of the UIST 2000* (pp. 91–100). San Diego, USA.

Hinds, J., & Joinson, A. (2019). Human and computer personality prediction from digital footprints. *Current Directions in Psychological Science, 28*(2), 204–211. https://doi.org/10.1177/0963721419827849

Hinds, J., Brown, O., Smith, L.G.E., Piwek, L., Ellis, D.A., & Joinson, A.N. (2021). Integrating insights about human movement patterns from digital data into psychological science. *Current Directions in Psychological Science, 31*(1), 88–95. https://doi.org/10.1177/09637214211042324

Hunkenschroer, A.L., & Luetge, C. (2022). Ethics of AI-enabled recruiting and selection: A review and research agenda. *Journal of Business Ethics, 178,* 977–1007. https://doi.org/10.1007/s10551-022-05049-6

Kock, N. (2005). Media richness or media naturalness? The evolution of our biological communication apparatus and its influence on our behavior toward e-communication tools. *IEEE Transactions on Professional Communication, 48*(2), 117–130. https://doi.org/10.1109/TPC.2005.849649

Kock, N. (2011). Media naturalness theory: Human evolution and behaviour towards electronic communication technologies. In S.C. Roberts (Ed.), *Applied Evolutionary Psychology* (pp. 380–398). Oxford University Press. https://doi.org/10.1093/acprof:oso/9780199586073.003.0023

Koeske, G.F., & Koeske, R.D. (1993). A preliminary test of a stress-strain-outcome model for reconceptualizing the burnout phenomenon. *Journal of Social Service Research, 17*(3–4), 107–135.

Lazarus, R.S. & Folkman, S. (1984). *Stress, Appraisal, and Coping.* Springer.

Marangunić, N., & Granić, A. (2015). Technology acceptance model: a literature review from 1986 to 2013. *Universal Access in the Information Society, 14*(1), 81–95. doi: 10.1007/s10209-014-0348-1

Marsh, E., Perez Vallejos, E., & Spence, A. (2022). The digital workplace and its dark side: An integrative review. *Computers in Human Behavior, 128,* 107118. https://doi.org/10.1016/j.chb.2021.107118.

Maurer, M., Bach, N., & Oertel, S. (2022). Forced to go virtual. Working-from-home arrangements and their effect on team communication during COVID-19 lockdown. *German Journal of Human Resource Management, 36*(3), 238–269. https://doi.org/10.1177/23970022221083698

Ore, O., & Sposato, M. (2021). Opportunities and risks of artificial intelligence inrecruitment and selection. *International Journal of Organizational Analysis, 30*(6). https://doi.org/10.1108/ijoa-07-2020-2291

Rab-Kettler, Karolina, & Lehnervp, B. (2019). Recruitment in the times of machine learning. *Management Systems in Production Engineering, 27*(2), 105–109.

Rafaeli, A., Ashtar, S., & Altman, D. (2019). Digital traces: New data, resources, and tools for psychological-science research. *Current Directions in Psychological Science, 28*(6). https://doi.org/10.1177/0963721419861410

Settanni, M., Azucar, D. & Marengo, D. (2018). Predicting individual characteristics from digital traces on social media: A meta-analysis. *Cyberpsychology, Behavior and Social Networking, 21*(4). https://doi.org/10.1089/cyber.2017.0384

Shaw, H., Ellis, D.A., & Ziegler, F.V. (2018). The Technology Integration Model (TIM): Predicting the continued use of technology. *Computers in Human Behavior, 83*, 204–214. https://doi.org/10.1016/j.chb.2018.02.001

Tippins, N., Oswald, F., & McPhail, S.M. (2021). Scientific, legal, and ethical concerns about AI-based personnel selection tools: A call to action. *Personnel Assessment and Decisions, 7*(2). https://doi.org/10.25035/pad.2021.02.001

van der Voet, J., & Steijn, B. (2020). Team innovation through collaboration: How visionary leadership spurs innovation via team cohesion. *Public Management Review, 23*(9), 1275–1294. https://doi.org/10.1080/14719037.2020.1743344

Vanden Abeele, M.M.P., Vandebosch, H., Koster, E.H., De Leyn, T., Van Gaeveren, K., Vicente et al. (2024). Why, how, when, and for whom does digital disconnection work? A process-based framework of digital disconnection. *Communication Theory, 34*(1), 3–17. https://doi.org/10.1093/ct/qtad016

Venkatesh, V., Thong, J.Y., & Xu, X. (2012). Consumer acceptance and use of information technology: extending the unified theory of acceptance and use of technology. *MIS Quarterly*, 157–178.

Walther, J.B. (1992). Interpersonal effects in computer-mediated interaction. *Communication Research, 19*(1), 52–90. https://doi.org/10.1177/009365092019001003

Walther, J.B. (1996). Computer-mediated communication: Impersonal, interpersonal, and hyperpersonal interaction. *Communication Research, 23*(1), 3–43. https://doi.org/10.1177/009365096023001001

Walther, J.B., & D'Addario, K.P. (2001). The impacts of emoticons on message interpretation in computer-mediated communication. *Social Science Computer Review, 19*(3), 324–347. https://doi.org/10.1177/089443930101900307

Wang, X., Cheng, M., Zhu, J., & Jiang, R. (2023). When texts meet emoji: A multi-stage study of tourism brands. *Journal of Travel Research*. https://doi.org/10.1177/00472875231203396

Ward, C., Harunavamwe, M., & Kanengoni, H. (2025). The influence of technostress creators on psychological, emotional, and social well-being of employees in digitised hybrid work settings. In: A. van Niekerk, N. Harry, & M. Coetzee (Eds), *Unlocking Sustainable Wellbeing in the Digital Age. Human Well-Being Research and Policy Making*. Springer, Cham. https://doi.org/10.1007/978-3-031-87616-5_8
Wildman, J.L., Thayer, A.L., Rosen, M.A., Salas, E., Mathieu, J.E., & Rayne, S.R. (2012). Task types and team-level attributes: Synthesis of team classification literature. *Human Resource Development Review, 11*(1), 97–129.
Würtenberger, A., Groneberg, D.A. & Mache, S. (2025). Digital stress perception and associations with work- and health-related outcomes among general practitioners in Germany: A quantitative study. *BMC Health Services Research 25*, 535. https://doi.org/10.1186/s12913-025-12653-5
Yam, J., & Skorburg, J.A. (2021). From human resources to human rights: Impact assessments for hiring algorithms. *Ethics and Information Technology, 23*. https://doi.org/10.1007/s10676-021-09599-7

Chapter 7

Forensic and investigative cyberpsychology

Outline and definition of the theme

Forensic or Criminal Psychologists might often undertake research and practice which typically provides insight into the intersection between psychology and the law. This might consist of using psychology to reduce bias, maintain fairness in the justice system, and understand factors that impact on eye-witness testimony. Additionally, those with clinical inclinations might also conduct evaluations of harm and risk, as well as ensuring competency of defendants and witnesses to appear in court. Aspects of the role might also include supporting victims, and developing or evaluating interventions designed to reduce criminal behaviour or impacts of crime.

In the case of forensic and investigative *cyber*psychology, this broadly is an intersection between forensic psychology, law, criminology, and cyberpsychology. The nature of the work might typically be more investigative such as informing cybersecurity, cyber-defence, digital investigation, threat detection, penetration testing, offender profiling, victim profiling/susceptibility, and surveillance. In terms of victim susceptibility, whilst there might be principles which apply from non-online crime, the digital environment has been found to increase risk of susceptibility. This is largely due to the fact that people are more likely to disclose more personal information online relative to physical settings, which increases the risk of them being subjected to social engineering, romantic scams, or phishing attacks (Walther & Whitty, 2021). As such, this indicates why cyberpsychology, and the study of people's behaviours relating to online cues and environments provides some nuance on understanding susceptibility in these

DOI: 10.4324/9781003581741-7

types of contexts (Whitty & Young, 2017). The subsequent sections provide detail on prominent issues or areas of work within this domain whereby cyberpsychology could be applied.

Conceptualising cybercrime

With additional contexts and capabilities that the Internet affords, this can bring opportunities for new or additional types of behaviour which, in some cases, might be antisocial or criminal. However, new criminal behaviours might occur at a rate beyond the capabilities of policies, professional training, and legal systems. As such, cyberpsychology evidence has the potential to be informative towards understanding what these cybercrimes are, characteristics associated with them, and potential impacts on individuals and society.

Within the academic literature, there is plenty of discussion about cybercrime typologies, particularly in relation to how these might be distinct from "real world" crime (Attrill & Wesson, 2019; Kirwan & Power, 2013). These broadly make distinction between crimes which are online-specific versus those which are online-enabled. Kirwan and Power (2013) for example note "internet-specific" crimes (e.g., malicious hacking, phishing), versus "internet-enabled" crimes (e.g., cyber-terrorism online group membership). Similarly, Gordon and Ford (2006) discuss type 1 (technological) versus type 2 (human element) cyber-crimes. Finally, Wall (2007) includes a third typology. As well as computer integrity crimes (e.g., attack network security, hacking) and computer-assisted crimes (identity theft), they also note computer-content rimes (e.g., illegal content online, online hate crime).

In relation to cyber-enabled crimes, this typically theorises that the internet enhances capacities to undertake criminal or illegal acts. In some cases, this might simply present perpetrators with additional contexts and opportunities such as undertaking acts of sexual harassment, stalking (cyberstalking) or engaging in extremist activities. As such, there are existing laws which apply irrespective of the context in which the behaviour has taken place. These types of crimes are often referred to being "old wine in new bottles". However, in the case of cyber-specific crimes, the behaviours which are undertaken are perhaps unique and distinct and so more difficult to underpin legally. These might include image-based sexual abuse (otherwise known as revenge porn), romance scams/online dating fraud, and malicious hacking. In these cases, cyberpsychology evidence which helps understand these behavioural components as distinct phenomena is clearly important. Additionally, evidence which helps understand the characteristics and factors associated with perpetration, as well as the impacts on victims, may help inform policies and procedures within legal, criminal justice, and victim support contexts.

There is a wealth of cyberpsychology evidence which has explored psychological harms associated with cybercrimes. For example, Mott et al. (2024) explored the impacts associated with organisational ransomware attacks. In addition to organisational-level impacts (e.g., financial and reputational) they found clear evidence of psychological harms associated with attacks, which ranged from emotional responses (e.g., anger and embarrassment), to more enduring experiences such as stress, post-traumatic stress disorder (PTSD), and even suicidal thoughts. Additionally, research on online scams has demonstrated long-term impacts associated with victimisation, such as severe psychological trauma (Button et al., 2025). As such a psychological angle on online cybercrime can be helpful to offer a victim-centred approach and therefore reduce impacts such as shame associated with victimisation and building resilience in organisational responding.

Case Study 17 introduces Jordon Kelly who is a Human Security Specialist, who helps organisations within cyber crisis management via training and simulation tools. This type of role can support organisations with enhancing their cybersecurity resilience, and importantly better equip and support staff in crisis response.

Case study 17 Jordon Kelly: Human Security Specialist

Qualifications

- MSc in Cyberpsychology
- MA in International Security
- BSc (Hons) in Forensic Psychology

How Jordon applies cyberpsychology

- Leading research and authoring of industry reports and white papers on topics such as human-centred security, addressing psychological vulnerabilities, futures threat forecasting and Zero Trust security strategy
- Developing unique and dynamic cyber crisis scenarios for global companies, designed to improve organisational resilience and enhance self-efficacy in senior leaders and executives
- Creating psychologically informed training and coaching content and consultancy offerings to help address human factors risk and improve organisational approaches to "security culture"
- Conducting qualitative and quantitative assessments of organisations' current approaches to human factors risk and delivered recommendations for development and improvement based on awareness, behaviour, and culture
- Pursuing research pathways exploring the topic of malign influence in the context of Authoritarian states, extremism, cults, and populist movements

More information: https://www.bps.org.uk/blog/careers-cyberpsychology-conversation-jordon-kelly

Characteristics associated with cyber-specific cybercrimes

Within the academic research, there is a strong focus on cybercrime both in relation to factors associated with victim susceptibility as well as characteristics of offenders/perpetrators. This is often in respect of cyber-specific crimes such as phishing, malicious hacking, and similar.

In respect of victim susceptibility, or profiles associated with victimisation, a recent review found that a large proportion of academic research has applied personality theory and Routine Activities Theory (Whitty, 2025) to understanding this. Personality characteristics which have been studied include impulsivity, internal focus of control, optimism, addictive personality, and low openness to experience (Whitty, 2025). For example, traits such as impulsivity (Hadlington, 2017; Kirwan et al., 2018; Price & Kirwan, 2013), fearful/anxious personality, neuroticism (López-Aguilar & Solanas, 2021), lower resilience (Papatraianou et al., 2014), and optimism bias have been noted as being higher risk in respect of cybersecurity victimisation. However, as well as personality traits, factors such as cognitive human factors have been raised in the literature as key risk factors. Work has often focused on the information processing and decision-making in respect of susceptibility to cybercrime, often in the context of cybersecurity. This can include things such as cognitive failures and biases (Hadlington, 2017; Hadlington & Murphy, 2018). For example, Hadlington and Murphy (2018) established that factors such as frequency of media multitasking and cognitive failures could predict engagement in risky cybersecurity behaviours. Some work in this domain has explored the level of processing which users might often afford to things like phishing emails, and noted that oftentimes it is a focus on more peripheral cues and more automatic, fast processing which is attributable to susceptibility rather than more deliberative processing of central informational content (Vishwanath et al., 2011, 2016). Models such as the Integrated Information Processing Model of Phishing Susceptibility (Vishwanath et al., 2011) and Suspicion, Cognition and Automaticity Model (SCAM; Vishwanath et al., 2016) help underpin the cognitive processing vulnerabilities which might exist here. This is all useful for providing psychologically informed awareness campaigns and training, designed around understanding key psychological factors associated with vulnerability, that might reduce subsequent cybersecurity vulnerabilities.

Next are some Case Studies which feature professionals who are focused on psychological correlates of cyber risk. Firstly, Case Study 18 introduces Anete Poriete who uses her cyberpsychology subject knowledge to research human experience factors such as cognitive biases and their implications for cybersecurity. Whilst this is more focused on user experience research, other Case Studies illustrate how professionals are using their subject knowledge within organisations. For example, Case Studies 19 and 20 introduce Lisa Ventura and Dr Erick Miyares who both detail extensive ways they apply cyberpsychology to a range of professional activities.

Case study 18 Anete Poriete: Lead Cyberpsychology and UX researcher

Qualifications

- Current: PhD Candidate in Information Security
- MSc in Security behaviour change module
- MSc in Cyberpsychology
- MA in Communications Management
- BSc in Business Psychology

How Anete applies cyberpsychology

- Researching into user experience in cybersecurity with focus on cyberpsychology
- Researching cognitive biases around cybersecurity perceptions
- Researching in digital product design implementing behaviour science principles

More information: https://www.linkedin.com/in/aneteporiete/

Case study 19 Lisa Ventura: Chief Executive and Founder of Unity Group Solutions Limited

Qualifications

- HND in Business and Finance
- Cyber security certifications

Networks

- Fellow – Chartered Institute of Information Security
- Member – British Computing Society
- Member – National Union of Journalists

How Lisa applies cyberpsychology

- Understanding human behaviour as the root of cyber risk: using principles of cyberpsychology to analyse how cognitive biases, social influence, and emotional triggers shape human decisions online. This helps design awareness and behaviour-change programmes that tackle the why behind risky behaviour, not just the what
- Bridging technology and human factors: integrating psychology with cybersecurity engineering, ensuring that awareness campaigns, training modules, and policy frameworks align with how people actually think, behave, and interact with systems, rather than how we expect them to
- Behavioural analytics and predictive modelling: applying cyberpsychological insights to AI-driven behavioural analytics, helping identify anomalies and intent in user behaviour. This supports early detection of insider threats, social engineering susceptibility, and burnout-related security lapses
- Designing emotionally resonant awareness campaigns: campaigns such as "Squish The Phish" and "Staying Secure: Everyday Habits That Make the Biggest Difference" use humour, storytelling, and relatable narratives grounded in behavioural science, leveraging emotional engagement to reinforce secure habits
- Combatting cognitive bias in cyber decision-making: incorporating bias-awareness training such as the optimism bias ("It won't happen to me") and authority bias ("It came from the CEO, so it must be real") into executive briefings and simulations to improve judgment under pressure
- Incident response through a psychological lens: within tabletop exercises, addressing not only technical responses but also the psychological impact of breaches including stress, panic, diffusion of responsibility, helping teams build cognitive resilience and improve communication in crises
- Building security culture through identity and motivation: using motivational psychology to shape security

culture, focusing on intrinsic motivators like pride, belonging, and mastery. This shifts users from compliance-based security to values-driven engagement
- Ethical AI and human-centred security design: exploring how AI systems can be designed with ethical, human-centred safeguards and embedding cyberpsychological principles into model governance, transparency, and accountability frameworks
- Championing inclusion and neurodiversity in cybersecurity: advocating for neuroinclusive environments where different cognitive styles are recognised as assets in threat analysis, pattern recognition, and creative problem-solving
- Applying behavioural science to policy and strategy: framing cyber risk as a behavioural challenge as much as a technical one, using behavioural economics and psychology to influence governance, communication, and leadership decision-making around cyber resilience

More information: https://www.lisaventura.co.uk

Case study 20 Dr Erick Miyares: Cyber Behavior Scientist at CEROeUM LLC and Senior Cyber Threat Advisor at Department of Defense

Qualifications

- PhD in Cyberpsychology
- M.S. in Cybersecurity
- B.S. in Cybersecurity

Networks

- Association of Threat Assessment Professionals (ATAP)
- Military Cyber Professionals Association (MCPA)

- Information Professionals Association
- Pat Tillman Scholar
- DoD National Defense Engineering and Science Graduate (NDSEG) Fellow

How Erick applies cyberpsychology

- Applying cyberpsychological frameworks to analyse the online behaviours and digital footprint of trusted employees, identifying psychological risk factors (e.g., stress, grievance, digital disengagement) that may lead to malicious or unintentional insider threats
- Conducting novel research into the psychological vulnerabilities exploited by highly emotive AI companions and the associated security risks posed by employees engaging in concerning, inappropriate, or unhealthy relationships with these services (e.g., adult fantasy, emotional over-dependence, mental health impact, and family issues)
- Investigating and developing countermeasures for the unauthorised use of public and personal AI services (e.g., ChatGPT) on government/organisational computers, specifically focusing on the psychology behind employees inappropriately "cut-pasting" controlled, sensitive, or classified materials into these tools
- Analysing how trusted employees may utilise both sanctioned and unsanctioned AI tools to engage in sensitive conversations regarding mental health or seek information on how to harm their organisation, leveraging AI's perceived anonymity/non-judgment to bypass traditional security controls
- Translating psychological insights on digital behaviour and AI interaction into actionable, human-centric security protocols, AI-governance policies, and effective training to enhance organisational cyber-resilience and reduce human-error-based data loss

More information: https://www.linkedin.com/in/erick-miyares/

It is noteworthy to mention that there is an observed mismatch between the academic cyberpsychological literature and real-world issues in this domain. Specifically, a majority of academic insight seeks to study cybercrime vulnerabilities/susceptibilities as well as associated impacts on the individual level. However, a significant focus in the sector and within organisations tends to be on how vulnerabilities need to be tackled and mitigated at an organisational level. Both perspectives are clearly critical, but it does create a degree of disconnect between research and practice, and therefore presents challenges to organisational practices being evidence-informed. Perhaps suitable ways to find synergy here are to integrate human factors perspectives which can account for things like individual differences, into the needs assessment, cybersecurity readiness and auditing, and/or cybersecurity training provision, which can provide this individual-level human insight into what are important organisational issues. Frameworks which draw on user attitudes, acceptance, locus of control or even personality, might be informative towards understanding personas of users, where more specified or targeted awareness or skills training might be beneficial. This could be somewhat complimentary to Cyber Assessment Framework (CAF) processes within needs assessment and auditing within organisations which can provide a parallel human factors needs assessment alongside the more technical and infrastructural components, and thus provide a more comprehensive and perhaps more robust cybersecurity assessment process. In summary, we need to train and support people psychologically, not just procedurally.

In relation to this issue, Case Study 21 introduces Todd Fletcher who is a Security Consultant who draws in cyber-behavioural analysis and insights to help security teams assess security systems.

Case study 21 Todd Fletcher: Cybersecurity Consultant at CrowdStrike

Qualifications

- MSc in Cybersecurity and Information Assurance
- Certified Information Systems Security Professional (CISSP) credential

- GIAC Security Operations Certified (GSOC)
- GIAC Cyber Threat Intelligence (GCTI)

How Todd applies cyberpsychology

- Interpreting technology-specific practitioner motivation, acceptance, and personality traits to clarify control adoption and operating behaviour to assist in security program improvements
- Applying demographic, skill-confidence, and self-efficacy indicators to tailor interventions, training, and change approaches
- Evaluating identity dynamics and community belonging to assess security culture and team cohesion
- Integrating cognitive, emotional, and stress-related factors to improve decision-making, reduce workload friction, and reinforce human–technology trust

More information: https://toddmfletcher.com/

Factors associated with perpetration

In relation to online offending behaviour, the focus is often on motivation, escalation, and behavioural patterns. In respect of offenders themselves, research has typically sought to characterise and profile cybercriminals (Bada & Nurse, 2021; Palmieri et al., 2021). This has included exploring personality trait characteristics and psychopathology which might be associated with cybercriminality (Woods, 2022). For example, cyberpsychology work suggests that psychopathy is a trait associated with cyberbullying, trolling, cyberstalking, online child pornography, and cyber fraud (March, 2022). In the case of juveniles, a recent meta-analysis exploring risk factors associated with cyberstalking, hacking, and sexting found that peer factors (e.g., deviant peers, peer pressure) were significant risk factors for all three behaviours and some indication that dark personality traits play a small role in determining cyberstalking and sexting (Wissink et al., 2023). Other research has sought to consolidate an explanation about how or why certain individual different traits might relate to cybercriminality. Palmieri et al. (2021) discussed this in respect of reinforcement sensitivity theory (RST; Gray, 1982, 1987) which refers to the behavioural approach and avoidance/inhibitory systems which regulate behaviour. These are the Behavioural Activation System (BAS) which underpin motivation towards action, and Behavioural Inhibition System (BIS) which explains avoidance or withdrawal away from action. Palmieri et al. (2021) found that BAS factors (Reward Interest, Goal-Drive Persistence, Reward Reactivity, and Impulsivity) have differential relationships with cybercrime, whereas BIS traits were all positively associated with cybercrime.

In respect of cyberthreats, Case Study 22 introduces Dr James McDowell who draws on cognitive-based principles to understand user-centred experiences of cyber-resilience.

Case study 22 Dr James McDowell: Executive Director at Cybercrime Research Unit

Qualifications

- PhD in Psychology
- M.S. in Cybersecurity
- M.S. in Data Analytics
- B.S. in Finance
- B.S. in Economics

How James applies cyberpsychology

- Identifying threat actor motivations to anticipate future threats
- Understanding cognitive biases and heuristics exploited by threat actors to mitigate cybercrime
- Using CBT principles to support survivors through victim-centred responses to cybercrime

- Analysing AI-enabled manipulation patterns to detect and defend against sophisticated attacks weaponising human psychology
- Teaching the next generation of cybercrime investigators victim-centred response techniques to enhance cybercrime reporting and survivor resilience

More information: https://www.cybercrime.institute/

Understanding attitudes and perceptions about cybercrimes

As well as exploring victim and perpetrator characteristics and experiences, cyberpsychology evidence has significant merit when understanding bystander attitudes and behaviour, especially when digital traces of previous behaviour can be utilised as a basis for exploring these issues. In the context of cybercrime, bystanders might play a fundamental role either in identifying acts and thus potentially being able to provide evidence as part of criminal convictions, or even intervening to prevent subsequent or ongoing action. Bystander attitudes have been studied in respect of image-based sexual abuse (Attrill et al., 2021; Mainwaring et al., 2024), to explore factors associated with intervening and the impact of victim characteristics in this regard (Mainwaring et al., 2024). In the case of "revenge porn", as a specific type of image-based sexual abuse, cyberpsychology evidence illuminates factors that relate to victim-blaming behaviour (Attrill et at., 2021). That is, using video recounts from victims, Attrill et al. (2021) found that more blame was attributed to victims when participants (i.e. bystanders) were indirectly asked who was to blame, rather than being asked directly. This might suggest that there are implicit processing biases at play when attributing blame. This indicates that there are key practical considerations to take forward with regards to criminal investigation and police questioning tactics which are sensitive to these potential biases. Beyond this, the wider cyberpsychological literature on image-based sexual abuse has afforded nuance on the various types of image-based sexual abuse, which helps better legal conceptualisation and practices in how they are dealt with (Fido & Harper, 2020; Rousaki & Fido, 2025), as well as education and awareness-raising literacy regarding this type of cyber-crime.

Clearly education and awareness-raising are important, especially when used as early intervention and behaviour change provision. Case Studies 23 and 24 introduce Dr Claire Sutherland and Nadine Rose-Smith who use cyberpsychology insights to inform policy, develop stakeholder online safety training, and inform behaviour change.

Case study 23 Dr Claire Sutherland: Cyber Safety Consultant at BCyberAware and Digital Schools Awards Scotland

Qualifications

- PhD in Psychology

Networks

- Chartered Member of the British Psychological Society (BPS)

How Claire applies cyberpsychology

- Delivering online safety workshops to students, staff, parents, and other professionals
- Developing and implementing anti-bullying and cyber safety policies in schools
- Writing for National Online Safety as a social media subject matter expert
- Conducting research on behalf of the Australian Government's eSafety Commissioner
- Assisting schools by promoting, recognising, and encouraging a whole school approach to digital technology use

More information: https://www.bps.org.uk/blog/careers-cyberpsychology-conversation-dr-claire-sutherland

Case study 24 Nadine Rose-Smith: Global Secure Behaviour Training and Engagement Lead at a large food and beverage organisation

Qualifications

- MSc in Occupational Psychology
- BSc in Psychology

How Nadine applies cyberpsychology

- Cyber security awareness and training
- Behaviour change to elicit positive and secure online behaviours
- Understanding our social interactions online and susceptibility to social engineering

More information: https://es.linkedin.com/in/nadine-rose-smith

Finally, Case Study 25 offers a different perspective from Dr George Raywood-Burke who is a Senior Scientist at Airbus and manages cybersecurity needs across the business. His focus on cyberpsychology-related education is more in respect of research and innovation within an organisation, alongside mentorship of junior cyberpsychology researchers.

Case study 25 Dr George Raywood-Burke: Senior Scientist in Human-Centric Security at Airbus

Qualifications

- PhD in Cyberpsychology and Decision-Making
- BSc in Psychology with Professional Placement

Networks

- Chartered Psychologist with the British Psychological Society (BPS)

How George applies cyberpsychology

- Leading and developing cyberpsychology research and innovation projects to support the cyber security needs across different areas of Airbus
- Collaborating with academia and other organisations to incorporate human-centric approaches to improving cyber security decision making
- Supporting PhD students and interns working within Airbus Cyber Innovation to have a positive impact upon cyber security posture
- Distributing findings through internal technical reports, and externally through publications and public events
- Providing recommendations for practice and future research directions on human-centric cyber security topics

More information: https://UK.linkedin.com/in/george-raywood-burke

Digital investigation

A prominent domain in which cyberpsychology could prove highly relevant is that of digital investigation. This can involve various types of investigation, some being *covert investigations* where covert operatives might engage with suspects with a view to eliciting enough evidence from them to be used to convict, and others being more *evidence-gathering investigations* which might be more commonly referred to as digital or cyber forensics. Digital forensics can consist of processes such as identifying, obtaining, analysing, and reporting digital evidence from digital systems or devices to support legal proceedings.

In either type of digital investigation, this might often involve operatives developing false personas to enable them to be covert either via active communication with suspects or to go undetected when accessing digital or online systems (e.g., the Dark Web etc). In either case, there is a clear need to ensure the integrity of one's covert identity to avoid being detected. The cyberpsychology evidence on digital traces and online identity can be especially helpful here to understand how cyber investigators might create a convincing identity which is associated with relevant person characteristics and does not "leak" traces which might otherwise raise suspicion. For example, in the case of covert investigation, if an operative was posing as a 13 year old girl on Instagram in an attempt to gather sufficient evidence to convict a suspected paedophile they were engaging with, they would benefit from evidence-based insight on what the behavioural markers are that might be related to the characteristics of a 13 year old girl. This might be related to the types of photos shared, liking behaviour, type of language used, engaging in relevant social media trends, following accounts of things a prototypical 13 year old girl might be interested in, and so on. The richer the persona in this regard, the more convincing this identity can be.

Digital traces could also be used from another perspective in respect of identifying suscepts based on fake or false personas they may have created. That is, cyberpsychological evidence provides insight into what online behaviours signal demographic or psychographic characteristics, which are identifiable even from very subtle or passive behaviours. As such, there may be "leakage" which can be detected here which gives cyber investigators an opportunity to identify and possibly convict suspects. This could equally be helpful in the scoping phases of evidence-gathering investigations when operatives are attempting to build up a profile of an individual and thus might benefit from cyberpsychology evidence to recognise how certain online identity markers and behaviours can be accurate in informing identity judgements.

Summary of key impacts of cyberpsychology

Here is a summary of the key impacts from these key themes in the research literature and Case Studies:

- **Supporting cybersecurity resilience** – cyberpsychology insights help understand human factors relating to resilient systems and culture

- **Understanding user factors and vulnerabilities** – cyberpsychology insights and behavioural analysis techniques help understand human factors associated with potential vulnerabilities in respect of victimisation and perpetration of cybercrime and cyber-threat
- **Supporting incidence response** – cyberpsychological insights can support cyber-threat incident responses beyond the more typical technical response requirements (e.g., understanding how to support victims or actors)
- **Raising cybersecurity awareness and education** – cyberpsychology insights can support evidence-based education and awareness-raising campaigns regarding cybersecurity

Advice

As work relating to forensic and investigative cyberpsychology can largely consist of working with law enforcement, and defence and security sectors, it is important to recognise that there will be rigorous vetting processes and security clearance protocols prior to any involvement in these domains. This might vary between nations, but in the UK the United Kingdom Security Vetting (UKSV) is the main UK government provider for these types of protocols. Vetting can take significant amounts of time, and might involve costs, so it is important to explore this in good time. If there are any criminal convictions or charges against you or a family member, these will likely restrict your clearance potential which might therefore prevent you from undertaking any work associated with national security or similar.

Additionally, as outlined in Chapter 3, it is important to ensure you translate your insights into language that makes sense to your target clients and groups. In the case of forensic cyberpsychology, the types of clients are likely to be include Government agencies (Military of Defence, Home Office, Defence Science & Technology Laboratory), cybersecurity technology companies or agencies, and legal services/law firms. Here are key areas which are worth doing some self-study on, to better understand the types of things that organisations will be interested in. Some of these might include:

- Supply chain attacks – attacks which target third-party vendors whereby any vulnerabilities which stem from this are introduced into an organisation's system

- Ransomware – a malicious software which blocks access to a system until a fee is paid to release the block
- Social engineering – tactics to manipulate or influence a victim to gain control over a system or steal information (e.g., can involve methods such as phishing)
- Insider threat – risks within an organisation where an employee or contractor misuses access to an organisations system or information which causes harm
- Human factors – understanding how humans interact with digital systems

Indicative keywords and job roles

- User Researcher
- Evidence Reviewer
- Project Officer/Coordinator
- Policy and Evaluation Officer
- Cyber Intelligence Officer
- Research Analyist
- Human Factors
- Behavioural Advisor
- Project Manager
- Digital Investigator
- Digital Traces
- Digital Forensics
- Digital Forensic Investigator
- Cyber Threat
- Cyber Forensics
- Threat Detection
- Cybersecurity
- Cyber Incident Response Analyst

Resources

CREST (Centre for Research and Evidence on Security Threats) – https://crestresearch.ac.uk/

Cyber Assessment Framework – https://www.ncsc.gov.uk/collection/cyber-assessment-framework

Department for Science, Innovation and Technology. Cyber Security and Resilience Bill – https://www.gov.uk/government/publications/

cyber-security-and-resilience-bill-policy-statement/cyber-security-and-resilience-bill-policy-statement

Europol Internet Organised Crime Threat Assessment (iOCTA) – https://www.europol.europa.eu/iocta/2014/appendix-3.html

Rephrain Network: a National Research Centre on Privacy, Harm Reduction and Adversarial Influence Online – https://www.rephrain.ac.uk/

UK Cyber Security Council: Digital Forensics – https://www.ukcybersecuritycouncil.org.uk/careers-and-learning/cyber-career-framework/digital-forensics/

United Kingdom Security Vetting (UKSV) – https://www.gov.uk/government/organisations/united-kingdom-security-vetting

References

Attrill, A., & Wesson, C. (2019). The Psychology of Cybercrime. In T.J. Holt & A.M. Bossler (Eds), *The Palgrave Handbook of International Cybercrime and Cyberdeviance*. Palgrave Macmillan.

Attrill, A., Wesson, C., Chater, M.L., & Weekes, L. (2021). Gender differences in videoed accounts of victim blaming for revenge porn for self-taken and stealth-taken sexually explicit images and videos. *Cyberpsychology Journal of Psychosocial Research on Cyberspace, 15*(4). https://doi.org/10.5817/CP2021-4-3

Bada, M., & Nurse, J.R.C. (2021). Profiling the cybercriminal: A systematic review of research. In proceedings of *2021 International Conference on Cyber Situational Awareness, Data Analytics and Assessment (CyberSA)* (pp. 1–8). Dublin, Ireland.

Button, M., Shepherd, D., Blackbourn, D., Sugiura, L., Kapend, R., & Wang, V. (2025). Assessing the seriousness of cybercrime: The case of computer misuse crime in the United Kingdom and the victims' perspective. *Criminology & Criminal Justice, 25*(2), 670–691. https://doi.org/10.1177/17488958221128128

Fido, D., & Harper, C.A. (2020). An introduction to image-based sexual abuse. In D. Fido & C. Harper (Eds), *Non-consensual Image-based Sexual Offending*. Palgrave Studies in Cyberpsychology. Palgrave Macmillan.

Gordon, S., & Ford, R. (2006). On the definition and classification of cybercrime. *Journal in Computer Virology, 2*(1), 13–20. https://doi.org/10.1007/s11416-006-0015-z

Gray, J.A. (1982). *The Neuropsychology of Anxiety: An Enquiry into the Functions of the Septo-Hippocampal System*. New York: Clarendon Press.

Gray, J.A. (1987). The neuropsychology of emotion and personality, In S.M. Stahl, S.D. Iverson, & E.C. Goodman (Eds), *Cognitive Neurochemistry* (pp. 171–190). New York: Oxford University Press.

Hadlington, L. (2017). Human factors in cybersecurity; examining the link between Internet addiction, impulsivity, attitudes towards cybersecurity, and risky cybersecurity behaviours. *Heliyon, 3*(7), e00346. https://doi.org/10.1016/j.heliyon.2017.e00346

Hadlington, L., & Murphy, K. (2018). Is media multitasking good for cybersecurity? Exploring the relationship between media multitasking and everyday cognitive failures on self-reported risky cybersecurity behaviors. *Cyberpsychology, Behavior, and Social Networking, 21*(3), 168–172. https://doi.org/10.1089/cyber.2017.0524

Kirwan, G.H., Fullwood, C., & Rooney, B. (2018). Risk factors for social networking site scam victimization among Malaysian students. *Cyberpsychology, Behavior, and Social Networking, 21*(2), 123–128

Kirwan, G., & Power, A. (2013). *Cybercrime: The Psychology of Online Offenders*. Cambridge University Press.

López-Aguilar, P., & Solanas, A. (2021). Human susceptibility to phishing attacks based on personality traits: The role of neuroticism. In Proceedings of *2021 IEEE 45th Annual Computers, Software, and Applications Conference (COMPSAC)* (pp. 1363–1368). Madrid, Spain. doi: 10.1109/COMPSAC51774.2021.00192.

Mainwaring, C., Scott, A.J., & Gabbert, F. (2024). Facilitators and barriers of bystander intervention intent in image-based sexual abuse contexts: A focus group study with a university sample. *Journal of Interpersonal Violence, 39*(11–12), 2655–2686. https://doi.org/10.1177/08862605231222452

March, E. (2022). Psychopathy: Cybercrime and cyber abuse. In P. Marques, M. Paulino, & L. Alho (Eds), *Psychopathy and Criminal Behavior* (pp. 423–444). Academic Press.

Mott, G., Turner, S., Nurse, J.R.C., Pattnaik, N., MacColl, J., Huesch, P., & Sullivan, J. (2024) "There was a bit of PTSD every time I walked through the office door": Ransomware harms and the factors that influence the victim organisation's experience. *Journal of Cybersecurity, 10*(1). https://doi.org/10.1093/cybsec/tyae013.

Palmieri, M., Shortland, N., & McGarry, P. (2021). Personality and online deviance: The role of reinforcement sensitivity theory in cybercrime. *Computers in Human Behavior, 120*, 106745. https://doi.org/10.1016/j.chb.2021.106745

Papatraianou, L.H, Levine, D., & West, D. (2014). Resilience in the face of cyberbullying: An ecological perspective on young people's experiences of online adversity. *Pastoral Care in Education, 32*(4), 264–283. https://doi.org/10.1080/02643944.2014.974661

Price, K., & Kirwan, G. (2013). Personality caught in the social net: facebook phishing. In A. Power & G. Kirwan (Eds), *Cyberpsychology and New Media: A Thematic Reader* (pp. 146–156). Taylor and Francis.

Rousaki, A., & Fido, D. (2025). Understanding image-based sexual abuse through Greek public and legal lenses: A constructionist thematic analysis. https://doi.org/10.31234/osf.io/b4fgc_v1

Vishwanath, A., Herath, T., Chen, R., Wang, J., & Rao, H. (2011). Why do people get phished? Testing individual differences in phishing vulnerability within an integrated, information processing model. *Decision Support Systems, 51*(3), 576–586. https://doi.org/10.1016/j.dss.2011.03.002

Vishwanath, A., Harrison, B., & Ng, Y.J. (2016). Suspicion, cognition, and automaticity model of phishing susceptibility. *Communication Research, 45*(8), 1146–1166. https://doi.org/10.1177/0093650215627483

Wall, D.S. (2007). *Cybercrime: The Transformation of Crime in the Information Age*. Polity Press.

Walther, J.B., & Whitty, M.T. (2021). Language, psychology, and new new media: The hyperpersonal model of mediated communication at twenty-five years. *Journal of Language and Social Psychology, 40(*1), 120–135. https://doi.org/10.1177/0261927X20967703

Whitty, M.T. (2025). A systematic literature review of profiling victims of cyber scams: Setting up a framework for future research. *Cogent Social Sciences, 11*(1), 2563781. https://doi.org/10.1080/23311886.2025.2563781

Whitty, M.T., & Young, G. (2017). *Cyberpsychology: The Study of Individuals, Society and Digital Technologies*. Wiley.

Wissink, I.B., Standaert, J.C.A., Stams, G.J.J.M., Asscher, J.J., & Assink, M. (2023). Risk factors for juvenile cybercrime: A meta-analytic review. *Aggression and Violent Behavior, 70,* 101836. https://doi.org/10.1016/j.avb.2023.101836.

Woods, N. (2022). Users' psychopathologies: Impact on cybercrime vulnerabilities and cybersecurity behavior. In M. Lehto & P. Neittaanmäki (Eds), *Cyber Security. Computational Methods in Applied Sciences* (pp. 93–134). Springer.

Chapter 8

Final remarks

General indicative contributions of cyberpsychology

Whilst I have offered indicative roles and job titles, alongside example sector challenges, which can help situate cyberpsychology's contributions within each chapter, I think it is useful to provide a more synthesised summary of the types of ways cyberpsychology roles can function across sectors. This synthesis is based both on the academic subject knowledge that is currently present in the literature, the example Case Studies, and how these align to be practically useful as career opportunities in sectors.

Drawing together Case Studies was illuminating about the type of domains which seem to be most prominent for those in cyberpsychological-related careers. Indeed, the greatest proportion appear to be occupied in forensic and investigative cyberpsychology, largely in cybersecurity domains. This is not surprising given the critical importance of this in society, but it was an interesting observation. Perhaps there is generally greater recognition of human factors in cybersecurity compared to other sectors or domains and more visibly relevant job roles and opportunities which explains this. However, I hope that this book might start to widen the recognition of how cyberpsychology can apply to a more diverse set of job roles and sectors, and prompt people to diversify their thinking of what opportunities there may be.

In general, I believe there are currently three prominent ways that cyberpsychology roles can be best realised. These are by being either i) an independent cyberpsychology consultant or business owner, ii) being a user researcher, or iii) being a Psychologist

DOI: 10.4324/9781003581741-8

via an established practitioner route who selects to use cyberpsychology-informed approaches or topics as their professional focus. Each of these is discussed in more detail below.

Independent cyberpsychology consultant and/or business owner

What is evident from the Case Studies throughout this book, is that many of these are consultant-type roles, and include those who have built their own business as a means of offering cyberpsychology-related services. There is significant merit to this given that the business and consultancy expertise can be built in a bespoke way to best match the individual's subject expertise and experience, as well as marketed to align with different types of sectors or organisational challenges. Such businesses can be situated according to current or future priorities relating to digital, and therefore offer viable services which might appeal to a range of client types.

Of course, building one's own business or indeed operating as an independent consultant can bring specific challenges, at least from the perspective of understanding the processes involved in business start-up and growth. This is why I have included some pragmatic considerations in Chapter 3 regarding some of these processes which I hope is at least a starting point to understanding how business start-up and ownership might operate.

Some of the specific types of consultancy projects which might be most relevant to cyberpsychology consultants include:

- Advising on governmental reviews, policy briefings, contributing evidence or reviews, and similar, which might inform policy or regulation relating to digital issues
- Advising public sector practitioners (e.g., health, education provides) or commissioners on how to apply cyberpsychology principles or frameworks in professional practice
- Advising digital technology providers on product development
- Contract research or evaluation work on understanding experiences or impact of digital use or engagement on users, clients or organisations
- Providing expert commentary in the media or for public-awareness campaigns relating to digital technology or the internet

- Writing blogs or public-friendly pieces for audience awareness or education on digital-related issues
- Consulting with organisations to help them solve a particular digital-related issue affecting employees or clients

User researcher roles

Unlike consultancy or business ownership, user researcher roles are much more established as roles within various sectors, including in the public sector (e.g., Civil Service), retail, communication and marketing, and more. As such, these roles are already situated within different types of sectors or organisations, to support user-centric perspectives relevant to the organisation's mission. This presents excellent opportunities for those interested in pursuing careers which apply cyberpsychology.

Of course, the specific reference point of what the research relates to will largely depend on what type of sector and organisation the positions are situated in, but largely, there will be key merits to cyberpsychology insights relating to digital use, user motivation, and behaviour which apply readily and widely. In addition, the more generic skills from psychology, relating to research enquiry (e.g., how to measure attitudes, scale development, develop interview agenda), and data analysis and interpretation (e.g., selecting appropriate analytic methods and techniques, interpreting statistics to draw conclusions), will be fundamentally relevant skills to bring to these roles.

Some of the specific types of tasks relevant to user researchers might include:

- Collaborating with digital technology developers on product development through conducting user testing and/or usability testing
- Selecting suitable methods for measuring or evaluating user experiences or impacts of digital use of specific products or services
- Selecting appropriate methods for undertaking market analysis or insights to better understand user groups and needs

Psychology Practitioner roles

Finally, I believe that another prominent means of developing a career using cyberpsychology is based on applying these insights within professional practice once in an established Practitioner Psychologist role. Whilst this is by no means an easy or accessible route for many, given the various years of training required, it does seem that this can be a credible means of applying cyberpsychology. Some of the Case Studies and discussions within chapters illustrate how this might be realised. However, these are just some examples which indicate how it may be possible to establish a credible career via a recognised route in psychology, via engaging in continued professional development (CPD) and scholarship relating to cyberpsychology to offer a more distinctive focus or specialism within the psychological services provided.

Some of the specific examples of how Practitioner Psychologists in various domains might apply cyberpsychology include:

- Clinical Psychologist – offering client consultations on things like cyber-trauma, digital use/overuse
- I-O/Occupational Psychologist – consulting with organisations on challenges such as distributed working or digital transformation
- Forensic Psychologist – consulting with organisations such as crime agencies, digital investigation teams or law enforcement on online offender profiling, or harms associated with victimisation
- Educational Psychologist – working with youth organisations or educational providers on reducing cyberbullying and associated harms, use of digital technology to support learning and educational practice
- Health Psychologist – consulting with health organisations or commissioners on utilising or evaluating digital health tools and services within healthcare and treatment plans

Broader considerations

Whilst being savvy with keywords and thinking outside the box is something we can all do when searching for cyberpsychology-informed careers, there are broader considerations which would significantly advance opportunities within cyberpsychology. Unfortunately, these are sector-level considerations which require larger infrastructural shifts to help the cause.

The first of these is to encourage recruitment agencies as well as large organisations such as Government agencies in the public sector, to start using keyword and filtering terms relating to "cyberpsychology" which can help increase discoverability of relevant roles. Currently, terms such as "digital" can be partially helpful, but might often draw up technical-related roles (e.g, data engineer, software developer) rather than something more angled towards the human aspect.

The second consideration relates to enhancing human-centric policy on issues such as cybersecurity when applied within organisations. If policy such as the UK Government Cyber Security and Resilience Bill (UK Government, 2025) included regulatory requirements for human-centric insights to be incorporated into assessment of cyber-risks alongside the more technical aspects of the Cyber Assessment Framework (CAF), organisations would have to do more to accommodate human factor perspectives and measurements into cybersecurity auditing and assessment. As such, this would most likely increase the demand for human factors and indeed cyberpsychology-informed roles to exist. The same applies to assessment processes at digital product and service procurement, whereby user-centric perspectives could be useful not only for assessing potential human related cybersecurity risks, but also might serve to support the adoption and integration of services more effectively.

A third consideration is about cybersecurity awareness training. There are wide debates about the effectiveness of current cybersecurity training provision, with prominent viewpoints that this is simply not fit for purpose. If awareness training providers included ways of assessing user characteristics, such as attitudes, locus of control, and personality, which cyberpsychology evidence suggests are important in determining vulnerabilities, this would offer more user-centric and personalised training opportunities which are designed towards specific types of persona groups, and thus might increase receptivity and effectiveness of training messages. This in turn would situate cyberpsychology specialists to be involved in the design and implementation of cybersecurity awareness training, rather than this remaining more exclusively in technical teams.

A final consideration relates to education and training. There needs to be an investment in interdisciplinary education and skills provision which draws together technical and human perspectives relating to design, implementation, and evaluation of digital technology and online engagement, so that we have people entering the workforce well equipped to handle roles which arguably benefit from more integrated knowledge. Without this, job roles will remain somewhat siloed into those which on one hand are purely technical (e.g., Data Engineer, Software Developer) and do not encompass user-centred or human perspectives, versus those which are psychological or behavioural (e.g., Behavioural Scientist), which have little insight into the specific back-end systems, or understanding of how to access and measure software interactions as a way to evaluate user behaviour. With greater integration comes greater insight into how one domain relates to another, so there can be more joined-up thinking and systems.

Clearly these are broader considerations which are not quick fixes, but I am hopeful that this book has provided an arsenal to equip those interested in pursuing cyberpsychology-informed careers to help navigate their place across different domains, sectors, and organisations.

Concluding thoughts

In gathering together some concluding thoughts, one prominent observation is that there are clearly many opportunities for those pursuing cyberpsychology informed careers, but perhaps the visibility of these needs a bit more work to make them more familiar and recognisable. One of the undercurrents of this book has been to provide pragmatic advice to help navigate this issue, and provide some synergy between the types of things that cyberpsychology people might know about, with the types of things that organisations and sectors care about, drawing in key Case Studies as concrete examples along the way. Of course, the domains and examples presented in this book are by no means an exhaustive list of how cyberpsychology-informed careers can be realised. However, I believe these are most likely to be the ones best aligned based on the prominent domains currently available in the cyberpsychology literature.

As cyberpsychology enthusiasts, we all have a role to play in raising the visibility, reputation, and utility of cyberpsychology, so it becomes more familiar and is perceived as more relevant to more sectors. This is not just about making the term more visible, but also requires proactive engagement of cyberpsychology academics and researchers to explain in lay terms how their insights are relevant, and engage in relevant networks to support this mission.

I don't ever see a time, at least in the near future, when cyberpsychology won't be relevant and so this offers an exciting time for us to work towards carving our contributions more solidly outside academic circles, to ensure that we can continue to enhance the way our work can be transformative on individuals and society.

References

UK Government (2025). *Cyber Security and Resilience Bill.* Retrieved October 17, 2025, from https://www.gov.uk/government/collections/cyber-security-and-resilience-bill

Index

Note: Page references in *italics* refer to the figures and **bold** refer to the tables.

For Product Safety Concerns and Information please contact our EU
representative GPSR@taylorandfrancis.com
Taylor & Francis Verlag GmbH, Kaufingerstraße 24, 80331 München, Germany

www.ingramcontent.com/pod-product-compliance
Lightning Source LLC
LaVergne TN
LVHW020910011026
849280LV00026B/304
* 9 7 8 1 0 3 2 9 4 7 7 4 7 *